Soul Survival

in a Corrupt and Anti-God World

Cristina E. Rodríguez

Copyright © 2003 by Cristina E. Rodríguez

Soul Survival
by Cristina E. Rodríguez

Printed in the United States of America

Library of Congress Control Number: 2002116436
ISBN 1-591602-96-3

All rights reserved. No part of this publication may be reproduced or transmitted in any form or by any means without written permission of the publisher.

All scripture refcrences in this book are taken out of the New International Version of the Life Application Bible. Copyright © 1991 by Tyndale House Publishers, and the New King James Version. Copyright © 1960.

Xulon Press
10640 Main Street
Suite 204
Fairfax, VA 22030
(703) 934-4411
XulonPress.com

To order additional copies, call 1-866-909-BOOK (2665).

Cristina Rodríguez
Box 5
Equality, IL 62434
cristina@soulsurvival.net

To my dear parents:
This is part of the fruit of your sacrificial labor of love in me. Thank you for walking through life with me and raising me in a Godly home where I always had the opportunity to do right.

And to my brothers and sis:
Joshua, Judah, Jordan, and Natalia. You're the best siblings on earth! (And the only ones I've got!)

Contents

Preface ix

1. Why Did God Create *You*? 11
2. The Answer to Life's Greatest Mystery 15
3. You…Fearfully and Wonderfully Made 29
4. Finding Your Identity in the Midst of a Generation Lost in Space 39
5. Restoring the Image 45
6. God Wants Me to Do…What With My Life???........53
7. The Great Go-Mission: Nine Tips in Accomplishing the Unfinished Task 57
8. Four Things We Are *All* Called to Do 95
9. Nine Ways To Find Your Specific Life Calling 111
10. Acquiring A Hunger and Passion for Christ 133
11. Daniel: The Chronicle of a Faithful Man of God 141
12. Six Things Leaders Look for in Youth 143
13. Satan's No. 1 Most Effective Strategy of Attack 163

14. Garbiology 165
15. The Drug Dilemma 171
16. Dating vs. Waiting: Which One Is God's Best? 179
17. Twelve Important Things Everyone Needs
    to Know About "Christian" Dating 181
18. And They Lived Happily Ever After…? 223
19. Wounds from a Friend or Kisses from
    an Enemy? 231
20. Taking Up The Martyrs' Torch Once Again 241
21. Catch the Vision! 249

A Big Thank You 259
About the Author 261

Preface

First of all I want to say a big "THANK YOU!" for taking time to read this preface! Not that it's *that* important, but just because most people don't!

Since I was little, I dreamed that I would someday write a book and become an author, and later as time went on, I purposed that it would be done before my twentieth birthday.

Before I began this book and the reason I did was because Christianity today has become so diluted and almost "deleted" especially among "Christian" youth. No high standards, no convictions, no difference from the world, no nothing that could really show that we are ambassadors from heaven to be salt and light to this world. So I asked God, "What is your heart for the generations of today? Do you have any special plans for us in the state we are now?"

All I wrote in this book is just what I feel God has spoken to my heart about what His heart is for this generation of today. It is all based on the unchangeable truth and immovable foundation of the Bible. All this is said simply in order to make clear what kind of book I was trying to write; not in the least to arrogantly say, "I have a lot I could teach you". No. I feel like the more I learn about God and as I walk this Christian life, the more I see just how ignorant and unlearned I am pertaining to the things of God. I've only just begun! And I've got a long way yet to go, but it's all so exciting!

Life for a Christian teen is no longer a playground. It's a battlefield out there. And if I've done my job right, this book can be like a tool or a compass to help you navigate through all these puzzling issues we go through. This life is a whole learning process and usually the hardest lessons we learn in life are the ones we thought we already knew.

All of life is about making decisions. And if reading this book has led you to make one wise choice in life, then it has been worth the two years I put into writing it! I want this book to motivate you to know, and love God and to stretch toward higher levels of spiritual maturity in your daily living and to begin fulfilling your God-given destiny right now!

1

Why Did God Create *You*?

The delicious molded Easter bunny lay in the brightly colorful basket surrounded by green paper "grass." With wide eyes glowing with excitement, the little girl carefully lifted the chocolate figure and gazed at it. She took a bite into one of its long ears. But after that sweet, creamy, chocolaty taste quickly faded, the little girl looked back at the candy in her hand. It was completely hollow! In such a shock she couldn't do anything but stare at it, the once highly prized treat in her hand.

This story is a brief, but sad analogy of how most of us experience life. We reluctantly grasp all the sweet, pleasurefull things this world has to offer, just to find nothing but emptiness, disappointment, and disillusionment. As the prophet Jeremiah said, we are always drinking from empty wells. We worship sports, clothes, food, new cars, jobs, relationships, but they all come up empty. Television keeps us craving while it sells us the latest fantasy to fulfil our every desire. Being marketed until we're numb, we race to the malls and worship before the "god" of materialism. But we just feel ripped off again. Because it doesn't produce anything. Our search leaves us scarred, guilty, and full of shame. We end up with a bigger emptiness than before. So we keep desperately searching. Like computer numbers falling in place, we are trapped in the deceptive matrix of life. Without the fulfilment, happiness or satisfaction we were searching for.

But does life have to be this way? Not at all! God created you for a purpose. But have you ever asked yourself *why?* Have you ever wondered about that? I mean, God didn't just create you to live, breath, wander, and roam around the planet!

I have asked this question to many, many people including "pseudo intellectuals" who know the answer to everything except the issues that really matter. They can tell you what the moon is made of, but they haven't the faintest idea what they are doing here on earth! They know what they are made *of*, but they don't know what they were made *for*.

I think this searching for a meaning to life has its root deep down in the fact that we are spiritually unfulfilled beings. Spirituality is something talked about a lot in today's modern world. Think about it. In the last few years, as never before, so many things about spirituality have come out in the secular world through movies, cartoons, commercials, music, publicity, jewelry, books, etc. But everyone is looking for what *they* call "spirituality". Many times they are finding the wrong kind.

People everywhere are looking for answers. With all the materialism that is in our world today, people have filled their lives with material things; but at the center of their being there is still a gaping hole. They've crowded their lives with "stuff" and then found out there is still an emptiness inside. So they started looking for other things. As I already said, we *are* spiritually unfulfilled beings when we just crowd our lives with material things. As humans we tend to live by feelings. People want those feelings of the supernatural. They will do anything and use anything they can to get that feeling, whether it's drugs, chants, hugging trees, images, anything that gives you those feelings.

It is so easy to wander aimlessly through life without giving any consideration to whether or not you are fulfilling your essential identity and purpose in life.

God created you for a close relationship with Him where Jesus is at the center and salvation is a definite truth rather than a feeling. You can't let your feelings and emotions shape your decisions. What should shape your decisions is who you are in God, what He is calling you to do, who He created you to be, what you are committed to, and what you stand for. Our world is changing more and more every day and we are going to have to learn to get better at changing faster and yet keep holding on to the core of what is really important—Jesus. And it is a fact that those people who are very sure about who that "unchanging core" is at the center of their being, are the ones who stay strong and persevere until the end.

The answer to realizing your potential and purpose in life, ultimately lies in understanding who you are in Christ. I feel this is a very important issue because we cannot fully experience a breakthrough in the Christian life and become more mature in our faith if there is a lack of understanding of our essential identity in Christ. Every human being that God ever formed was created by Him for a special purpose and destiny. It does not matter where you came from or how. This search leads us to discover the answer to life's greatest mystery. So let the fun begin! Excitement is in the air!

2

The Answer to Life's Greatest Mystery

All humanity, since the beginning of the world, either consciously or sub-consciously, has one supreme desire within its being—to know and understand the answers to "Who am I?", "Why am I standing here on earth?", "What is the point of life?", and "Where am I heading?" "What does Christianity have to do with life today?", "Does it really matter what I believe?"

Have you ever asked yourself any of those questions? Could it be possible that the emptiness that all humanity has long ago accepted as a natural part of the human condition is really a longing for the one, true God?

Leo Tolstoy, the great Russian intellectual who majored on many religious and philosophical issues, spent his whole life looking for the answer to the question: "Is there any meaning in my life that will not be destroyed by my death?" Although he had a permanent place in the annuals of world literature, yet his achievements were not enough to give his life meaning and he came to believe that he had accomplished nothing in life.

Many people have decided that they don't have the answer to life, so they just push this question out of their minds. But one of the saddest things I believe anyone could do with their life is to go through all of it and miss the whole point. A wise man once said, "All men should strive to learn before they die, who they are, where they are going, and why."

It has been well said that "religion" is man's way of trying to deal with his sin and guilt. Different religions have different ways of attempting to rid themselves of sin and its consequences. They may practice fasting, prayer, good works, dietary restrictions, or lying on beds of nails, and denying themselves legitimate pleasures or chastening themselves, often to a point of inflicting pain.

If you ask the average person he will probably tell you that he has gone to church sometime or another in his life, but it probably seemed to him as a ritual with no meaning. Many times I believe it is because of an ignorance or lack of understanding of the things of God, who God is, and really what Christianity is all about. I am aware that even for many Christians today, when it all boils down to the very essence of Christianity and what it is all about, it would be difficult to give an answer. I was that way even many years after I had given my life to Jesus. Yes, I was a faithful church-goer, and I did everything else you can think of to be a "good Christian", but if ever someone were to come up to me and ask me to really explain Christianity, I wouldn't have anything to say! I just really didn't get it either!

One friend I talked to, said to me, "Before I had an experience with God, church seemed empty, as if God had left the church, and it really didn't seem to matter to anyone." There was even an article that came out in Great Britain entitled, "God to leave the Church of England". The article went like this: "Following the precedents set by former Anglicans, God has indicated that He too is to leave the Church of England. According to some friends of God and other sources close to God, He has been unhappy for some time because of the direction the church has been taking, and has now finally had enough. One spokesman said, "Losing God has been a bit of a blow, but it's just something we're going to have to live with."

Many times people say that they can't believe in something that they haven't seen. But the truth is, we believe in many things that we can't see. Have you ever seen the wind? Have you ever seen history? Have you ever seen your brain? We see the effects of the wind, but the wind is invisible. We have records of history, but it is by "faith" we believe that certain historical events happened.

It has been well said, that an atheist can't find God for the same reason that a thief can't find a policeman. The fact of the existence of the Creator is self-evident. That's why the Bible says in Psalms 14:1, "The *fool* has said in his heart 'there is no God'. (My italics)

Each one of us is born with a sin nature, and it creates a barrier between humanity and God. As the scriptures say, "There is none righteous, no, not one." You could say, "Well, but I'm a good person."

Imagine you are filling out an application for your reservations in heaven. After filling out your name and address, phone number, etc., you come to a line marked, "Qualifications" What would you put there? "My belief in an existing God? All the "neighbors" I helped while on earth? The "good" life I have lived?

Or would you have to write, "No qualifications at all, other than my having received the free gift of salvation, paid for by the shed blood of Jesus Christ, on the cross." According to the most read, published, and widespread book on earth, *no one* qualifies for heaven by trying to be "good".

Mahatma Ghandi said, "It is a constant torture to me that I am still so far from Him whom I know to be my very life and being. I know it is my own wretchedness and wickedness that keeps me from Him."

Charles Spurgeon, the Prince of Preachers said, "Morality may keep you out of jail, but it takes the blood of Jesus Christ to keep you out of Hell."

Romans 3:23 tell us, "For *all* have sinned and come short of the glory of God." You could say, "But I have never really sinned."

Then let me ask you this: Have you ever told a lie? Even a tiny, white lie or a fib? Have you ever stolen anything? Even a tiny piece of candy, pen or a paper clip? Have you ever dishonored your parents? Even in a small word, thought or deed? Then you have already sinned and broken some of God's laws.

But so many times we compare ourselves with others and think, "Well yes, I've sinned a little, but just look at *him, he is worse!*" Let's imagine there is a pillar in front of you, that represents a scale of everybody who has ever lived. At the top is the very best person who has ever lived, and at the bottom is the worst person who ever lived. Who do you think you would put at the very bottom? Some people would probably say, "Adolf Hitler", or someone else they didn't like. Who would you put at the top? Some people would probably say, "Mother Teresa", or their own mother, or someone who they thought was the best person in the world. I don't know where on the scale you would put yourself, but I think I would put myself about in the middle. But now let's ask ourselves, what is the standard for this scale? Some may say, "Probably the standard is the ceiling." And that's where we get to the point. Seeing the big picture, the standard is not the ceiling, but the sky, and compared to that, all of us fall a long way short. You can compare yourself with others and you may fare well, but when you compare yourself to

The Answer to Life's Greatest Mystery

the true "standard" which is Jesus Christ, we all "fall short."

Millions of religious people are striving to be good, thinking that will merit their entrance into Heaven. In essence they are trying to purchase everlasting life by offering their "good deeds" to God as an exchange.

Salvation is about a relationship between you and God and that's why you could be a pastor or a pastor's kid, grow up in a Christian home, play some instrument on the church's worship team, or never miss a single meeting at church. You could be a missionary's kid. Bringing souls to their Savior is something you do all the time. You could hear all the sermons ever preached, read as many Christian books you can, and still not be saved. *Your circumstances won't ever make you saved.* And sadly there are many going to Hell, for this same reason, they think their circumstances will save them. I am a missionaries daughter, yet before I became a Christian, I was a rebel and prodigal in my heart.

You might have thought that maybe God will *overlook* your sins. Maybe He, in his mercy, could just look the other way. If He did, then He would be unjust. Think of it in connection with civil law. Can a judge look the other way when a criminal is obviously guilty, and stay true to what is right? Even if the judge feels sorry for the criminal, he must stay true to the law. Justice must be done. So should God overlook your crimes on Judgment Day? Should He turn a blind eye and compromise Eternal Justice? Or are you saying that God should just punish other people's "serious" crimes? But your lying and stealing and adultery of the heart *are* serious in His sight!

What then is the punishment for sin? It is everlasting damnation in Hell. You could say, "Oh that just a bunch of junk to try to scare me. I don't believe in Hell." Hebrews 9:27 warns us saying, "...it is appointed unto men once to die, but after this the judgment." There is no purgatory, no second chance, no other name, no other hope, and no other way for you to be saved. If you don't believe it this side of the grave, you will on the other.

After the terrorist attack in New York on September 11th, Hillary Clinton, senator of New York, commented on national television in regards to her first sighting of all the death and destruction. She said, "I think that this must be something that Hell is like." Believe it or not, the worst pain or suffering you can ever experience on this earth is but a speck of dirt compared to the everlasting punishment of Hell. It is an abode of darkness, depression, and despair. A terror-filled place, where murders, rapists, those who have tortured, lied, stolen, hated, been greedy, lustful, envious, jealous, blasphemous and rebellious will dwell.

It will be a place of "weeping and gnashing of teeth", a place where death will not bring welcome relief to suffering. Hell is the place where sinful humanity will receive its just rewards for crimes against the Law of a holy God.

But thank God, Christianity doesn't end there. It's good news! The "Good News" of the Christian faith is that no one need suffer the pains of religious works to get to Heaven. Christianity is principally about relationships rather than rules. It revolves around a Holy Being, the Almighty God rather than a religion or philosophy. Because Jesus took your punishment upon Himself at the cross, His blood can cleanse your conscience from the "dead works" of religion. He can free you from the torture of guilt.

Ephesians 2:4-9 says, "...for by grace ye are saved through faith; and that not of yourselves." I once heard a story about a man who died and went to heaven, and an angel met him at the Pearly Gates. "Here's how it works," the angel said. "You need 100 points to make it into heaven. You tell me all the good things you've done and I'll give you a certain number of points for each item, depending on how good it was. When you reach 100 points, you can get in." "Ok," the man said. "I was married to the same woman for

The Answer to Life's Greatest Mystery

50 years and never cheated on her, even in my heart." "That's wonderful!" the angel replied. "That's worth three points." "Three points?" the man responded. "Well... I attended church all my life and supported its ministry with my tithe and service." "Terrific!" the angel said. "That's certainly worth a point." "One point?!" the man complained. "Well, I also started a soup kitchen in my city and worked in a shelter for homeless veterans." "Fantastic...that's good for two more points." the angel announced. "Two points?!" the man exclaimed. "At this rate, the only way I get into Heaven is only by the grace of God!" "Bingo!" the angel exclaims, "100 points! Come on in!"

But what exactly is this word "grace?" Lets make an analogy of grace as being like when a father disciplines his son. I think we can all relate to it this way because I'm sure all of us have gotten a spanking at sometime or another when we were young! Suppose that this little boy has done something he knows is wrong and worthy of a spanking. Daddy calls him and asks him what he's done wrong. He tells it all and knows and dreads what's coming. Daddy gets out the paddle, and takes his son to another room, then Daddy raises the paddle and just as he is about to swing...he stops. And instead of bringing down the paddle to spank...Daddy says one word, "Mercy". And the little boy cries, "Oh thank you Daddy! Thank you Daddy! I love mercy!" You see, mercy is *not* getting what you deserve. If God would have rewarded us according to our sins...what might have become of us? But no, God is a God of mercy. So then Daddy says to his son, "Do you like mercy? Then you'll like grace even better. Here, take this extra dollar, go buy yourself some ice cream." The little boy cries, "Oh I don't deserve this Daddy!" Daddy says, "No, because that's what grace is all about."

Grace is getting what you *don't* deserve. If God were to give us grace according to our own merits, it would not be grace. Grace is the *unmerited* and *unearned* kindness, mercy, and forgiveness of God. That's why your salvation is not earned by works. No works are good enough! It's just by mercy and grace. Even when you cannot begin to think that He can use you, when you feel like you have failed Him most miserably, remember this, He can take the broken pieces—if you let Him, and He will make something beautiful out of them. This is the work that gives Him the most joy—restoring life to that which seems impossibly out of reach. Forgiving the unforgivable, and loving the unlovable.

On July 31, 1941, a prisoner escaped from the Auswitch concentration camp in Nazi Germany. As a reprisal, the Gestapo selected ten men totally arbitrary and they said that these ten men were going to be left to die of starvation in an underground bunker. One of these men who was selected, was a man named Francis Gagonistic. As this man was called out, he cried out, "Oh, my poor wife and children!" At that moment, another man who had been watching, stepped forward and he said, "My name is Maximilian Colby, I'm a Catholic priest, and I want to die instead of this man." His offer was accepted and he was taken down along with the others to that starvation bunker. He was such a remarkable man, he got them all singing and praying, and the spirit of the atmosphere was just glorious, just like in a church. In the end, they gave him a lethal injection to kill him.

On October 10, 1982, in St. Peters Square, Rome, Maximilian's death was put into right perspective, because present in a crowd of about one-hundred thousand people, was standing Francis Gagonistic, who was the man he had saved, along with his wife, his children, and his grandchildren. They were the many, who had been saved, by one man's sacrificial death.

That's exactly what Jesus did for you, He died as your substitute. He died... "To open their eyes, and to turn them from darkness to light, and from the power of Satan unto God, that they may receive forgiveness of sins..." —Acts 26:18 He died to give you life, to rescue you from the death penalty, which is the consequence for the things you do wrong. To set you free so that this barrier between you and God is removed, and you are free to have this relationship with God, and you are free to begin to change into the person that deep down inside, you were meant to be. And that is the good news of Christianity!

In John 6:35, Jesus said, "I am that bread of life; he that cometh to me shall never hunger and he that believeth on me shall never thirst." Jesus is the only one who can satisfy that deep hunger for truth that is in every human heart.

A Japanese girl explained it like this, "In Japan, it's as if we have two stomachs, one for ordinary food like fruit, vegetables, and meat, and another for rice. And no matter how much ordinary food we eat, we never feel full unless we eat rice, and then we're satisfied."

I think if Jesus would have been speaking to the Japanese, He would say, "I am the 'rice' of life. I am the one person who can satisfy this other stomach." All the other things in life like jobs, music, money, friends, sports, success, etc. can be good things and can only fill this one "stomach" but not the other. We can have a lot of fun with these things, but when its over, there is always a feeling that something is missing.

Why is Jesus the only one who can satisfy this other "stomach"? One reason I have found is this: He satisfies the hunger that is in every human heart for some meaning and purpose in life. The whole point in life is that we experience a relationship with God through Jesus Christ, and that is the only thing that truly satisfies. I am not saying that a life *without* Christ is not fun and exciting. It just does not fulfill It does not fill that other "stomach". And it's not just that Christianity is wonderful for people who kind of need that sort of thing, and if you have this gap in your life, you need Christianity, but if you don't have that gap, you don't need it. Christianity is public truth. If it's true for anyone-it's true for everyone. If it isn't true for anyone, it isn't true for everyone.

C.S. Lewis once said, "Christianity is a statement which, if false, is of no importance at all, and if true, is of infinite importance. The only thing it cannot be, is moderately important." So, since Christianity is true, then your Eternal destiny depends on how you respond to Jesus Christ. I don't want to change your religion, I just want Jesus to be real for you. I want you to discover Christ for yourself.

John 3:16 says, "God so loved the world that He gave His only begotten Son that whosoever believeth in Him shall not perish but have eternal life." At the very heart of Christianity is this: God loved the world so much, that He did something about it. He sent the only Son He ever had, Jesus Christ, to die on the cross for you and for me. And on that cross, Jesus took upon himself, everything that you ever did wrong, and everything you ever will do wrong, and He said, "Because I love you, so much, I don't want you to suffer for those things, and I will take them Myself. I will suffer in your place, I will die in your place." Salvation is a gift, not a reward. Salvation is free, but it wasn't cheap. Is your own heart so hard that you can't hear the nails being driven into the hands of Jesus and not be moved by such love? Isn't there a cry in your own heart, as you hear the agonies of the Cross? Or have a you a heart of stone? Please, come to your sense and obey the Gospel.

"For God sent not his Son into the world to condemn the world; but that the world through him might be saved." — Romans 3:17

This is the extent of God's love for you and me, that He would die for you even if you were the only person on the face of this earth! Just as with some intricate thing that you made, you wouldn't want your younger siblings to come and destroy it, God didn't want his own creation to be destroyed, so He asked His son, His only son, to come in the form of a man, a human being, and with his life pay the price for you, thousands of years before you were even born. Jesus Christ longs for that deep, intimate relationship with you, He longs for you to be in love with Him just as He is with you. Just like the love between a husband and wife, the husband expects his wife to return that love, attention, and devotion. Likewise, God wants you to wholeheartedly and single-focused, seek His face and return that great, unconditional love He showed in laying down His life just for you at the cross. With His blood He bought you, and paid the price for your soul, He forgave you and created you to fulfill a purpose in life.

A common excuse for some people not to receive Jesus is, "I'm not ready", "I'll do it later", or "I will wait until I am older and then I will get right with God." You may not get the chance. God may just lose patience and end your life in one second.

John Tillotson said, "He who provides for this life, but takes no care for Eternity, is wise for a moment, but a fool forever."

To say, "I hope I'm a Christian" or "I hope I go to Heaven", is like standing atop a skyscraper building, getting ready to bungee-jump and answering, "Do you have your bungee securely tied?" with, "I hope so." You want to *know* so, and you can, simply by obeying the Gospel.

Jesus warned that if we "jump" into death without Him, we would perish. Our great problem is a law that is even harsher than the law of gravity. It is the Law of an infinitely Holy and just Creator. He is not wise who thinks that he can outwit his Creator, enjoy a lifetime of sin, and repent at the last minute. Deathbed repentance is very rare. Most people think that God's patience is eternal. It is evidently not. This life you are living right now is not the end. There is life beyond the grave. History is not empty or meaningless. There is a coming Day of Judgment when God will give everlasting life or everlasting punishment to humanity.

Now you know the way to receive the everlasting life, but this decision is between you and God. I *urge* you to repent and cry out to God for forgiveness from your sins and ask Him to give you a new life! Because the longer you put it off, the harder it becomes and the more you will miss out. If you know your life is not right with God, if you would die today and are not sure where you are going, don't wait, have a talk with Him and get it right, now. You don't know how many days you have left living in this world before heading out into Eternity. You may never wake up tomorrow. Live every day as if it was the last one. Don't blow it for Eternity. Listen, believe and obey.

Maybe you have already taken this step and you could say, "Well how can I be *sure* that I'm saved?"

A two-year-old boy was once staring at a heater, fascinated by its bright orange glow. His father saw him and warned, "Don't touch that heater son. It may look pretty, but it's hot." The little boy believed him, and moved away from the heater. Some time later, when his father had left the room he thought to himself, "I wonder if it really is hot." He then reached out to touch it and see for himself. The second his flesh burned, he stopped *believing* it was hot. He now *knew* it was hot! He had moved out of the realm of belief into the realm of experience! Most people will say they "believe in God" (even the devil believes in God). However, when you *obey* the Word of God, turn from your sins and embrace Jesus Christ, you have stopped simply believing. The moment you reached out and touched the heater bar of God's mercy, you moved out of *belief* into the realm of *experience*. This experience is so radical, Jesus referred to it as being "born again".

The Answer to Life's Greatest Mystery

"Therefore if any man be in Christ, he is a new creature: old things are passed away; behold all things are become new." —2 Corinthians 5:17

Suppose two men walked into the room just after that child had burned his hand on the heater. One was a heater manufacturer and the other a skin specialist. Both assured that boy that he couldn't possibly have been burned. But all the experts, theories, equations and arguments in the world will not dissuade that boy, because of his experience.

Those who have been transformed by God's power need never fear scientific nor any other argument, because the man with an experience is not at the mercy of a man with an argument.

You can ignore this and shut out my voice, God's voice, the Bibles voice, or your own conscience's voice, but please listen to the voices of those who have died without Jesus. You can read the book of Ecclesiastes, written by one of the wealthiest, wisest man who ever walked the face if this earth, and one of the things he said was, "It is better to go to a house of mourning that to go to a house of feasting, for death is the destiny of every man; the living should take this to heart." -Ecclesiastes 7:2

But why does he say it is better to go to a place like a funeral, than to a party? Because people there are thinking on the things of Eternal value. Everything you attain outside of the kingdom of God will be torn from your hands by death. But why does someone have to die before people will begin thinking on Eternity? Now, while you are able to move and speak, give yourself to that which is Eternal. Ask God to make himself real for you. "For what is man profited, if he shall gain the whole world, and lose his own soul? Or what shall a man give in exchange for his soul?" —Matthew 16:26

Think of your life in about sixty years…will the life you are living now, count for Eternity? So many people one their deathbeds think back on their life with memories of total sadness because they can't say that they have done anything that will count for Eternity. It doesn't matter where you go or what you do, until you totally give your life over to the One who, with His blood, paid the price for your soul, you will never find fulfillment or purpose in life. Christianity is not boring, untrue, or irrelevant, it is all about living your life to the full!

Harsh though this first chapter may seem, it is my deepest desire that you will receive this in a spirit of gentleness on my part because I have poured my heart out to you. So thank you so much for taking the time to read this chapter. My primary motivation for writing it is a concern for your eternal salvation. I earnestly hope that you have made peace with God and discover "...the mystery that has been kept hidden for ages and generations, but is now disclosed to the saints. To them God has chosen to make known among the Gentiles the glorious riches of this mystery, which is Christ in you, the hope of glory." —Colossians 1:26-27

3

You...Fearfully and Wonderfully Made

"**I** praise you because I am fearfully and wonderfully made; your works are wonderful, I know that full well." —Psalms 139:14

Michelangelo Buonarotti, perhaps the greatest artist in history, painted the famous Sistine Chapel to retell Genesis' story of creation. He had six thousand square feet of ceiling to cover-the size of four average house roofs. If you have ever painted a ceiling with a roller, you know the difficulty of the task! But Michelangelo's plan called for 300, separate, detailed portraits of men and women! For over three years, he devoted all his labors to the exhausting strain of painting the vast overhead space with his tiny brushes. Standing on a huge scaffold, a paintbrush in hand, he painted while lying on his back, with his nose inches from the ceiling.

In the long days of summer, he had light enough to paint up to seventeen hours a day, taking food and chamberpot with him on the 60-foot scaffold. For thirty days at a stretch he slept in his clothes, not even taking off his boots. Paint dribbled into his eyes so he could hardly see. Freezing in the winter, and sweating in the summer he painted until at last the ceiling looked like a ceiling no more. He had transformed it into the creation story, with creatures so real, they seemed to breathe. But, as Michelangelo knew very well, his masterpiece was a poor, dim image of what God created.

There is no question as to whether or not God exists, but if there is a God, then we should be able to prove His existence without using "faith".

Imagine that you and I won a trip to Italy (that would be nice!) and we went to the Sistine Chapel. Suppose you had never seen anything like it and you said, "Wow! Who painted this?" And I said, "Oh it wasn't made, it just kind of fell together after billions of years. You know, paint just happened to fall from the sky, land on this building, soak through the ceiling, and form itself into these 300 human paintings you see." Would you believe me? Do you know of any building that didn't have a maker? Could I convince you of that? No! Because if something is designed, there must be a designer. Am I right? Everything you can see around you has had a maker. To believe anything else, that it happened by chance, is to have severe "brain damage"! *To say that there is no Creator is the very same thing!*

But how can you *know* that it had a maker? You can't see him, hear him, touch him, taste him or smell him. So what proof is there that there was a painter? The building itself is proof that there is a builder. Things that are made tell us there was a maker, and you don't have to have "faith" to believe in the maker, all you need are eyes to see and a brain that works. (But…if you want to approach the builder to do something for you, *then* you need to have faith in Him).

Exactly the same thing applies to the existence of God. How can we know there is a God? Lets say you can't see him, hear him, touch him, taste him or smell him. *Creation* alone tells us there is a Creator.

God spoke, and galaxies whirled into place, stars burned in the heavens and planets began orbiting their suns. He spoke again and the waters and lands were filled with plants and creatures running, swimming, growing, and multiplying the earth. He created this universe with such perfection that if the earth were any closer or farther away from the sun, moon, stars, and other planets, then life on this earth would be non-existent.

He created more stars in the skies than all the grains of sand in all the beaches in the world...and the most powerful of all telescopes reveal that there are so many stars in the Milky Way Galaxy alone that it would take a person four thousand years just to read their names, if he read them at the rate of one name per second! Yet God *does* call them by name! And each one of them is a different masterpiece of His.

This great, Almighty God who with just the word of his mouth created such a beautiful masterpiece as this universe, but...when it came to making man,"...the Lord formed the man from the dust of the of the ground and breathed into his nostrils the breath of life, and the man became a living being." —Genesis 2:7

Today we hear many arguments that God's spirit is in everything: the trees, the rocks, the grass, etc. Obviously not. God formed man from the dust of the ground and "breathed into his nostrils the breath of life, and man became a living being." He didn't breath His breath of life into the trees and rocks and grass. He *spoke* and all that was formed. God spoke the world into existence...but He reserved His very breath for man. When it came time to create man, it was different. It was special. It was unique. He didn't just speak and you were done, God wanted to have His hands in your making. He intricately formed every part of you; not just Adam and Eve, but *you*. Then He breathed

His breath of life into you to make you a living soul!

"My substance was not hid from thee when I was made in secret...thine eyes did see my substance, yet being unperfect; and in thy book all my members were written which in continuance were fashioned, when as yet there was none of them." —Psalm 139:15-16 In the beginning, someone thought about you, and even wrote a book about you. It was God. Isn't that incredible?! You and me, each one of us is a different work of art of God, He knit you together in the womb, and He already knew who you were even before you started to live this life!

Over fifteen centuries ago, Saint Augustine, the Bishop of Hippo quoted, "...men go forth to wonder at the heights of the mountains, the huge waves of the sea, the broad flow of rivers, at the vast compass of the ocean, the courses of the stars; but they pass by themselves without wondering."

Grab a mirror and take a good look at your eye. Did you know that your eye has 40,000,000 nerve endings, the focusing muscles move an estimated 100,000 times a day, and the retina has 137, 000,000 light sensitive cells. Charles Darwin himself said, "To suppose that the eye could have been formed by natural selection, seems I freely confess, absurd in the highest degree."

So if a man cannot begin to make a human eye, then how could anyone in his right mind think that eyes formed by mere chance? Yet, the eye is only a small part of the most sophisticated part of creation-the human body.

George Gallop, the famous statistician said, "I could prove God statistically; take the human body alone; the chance that all the functions of the individual would just happen, is a statistical monstrosity."

Did you know that your body is composed of the same nonliving chemical elements that make up the dust you see on the ground itself?! "...for dust you are and to the dust you will return." -Genesis 3:19 Check out these amazing facts

You...Fearfully and Wonderfully Made

about our human anatomy. (See, I *did* pay attention in science class!)

Sixty-five percent of our body's weight is Oxygen, eighteen percent is Carbon, ten percent is Hydrogen, three percent is Nitrogen, two percent is Calcium, and one percent is Phosphorus (there are some more elements which are extremely important but they are a very small minimum). Even though there are ninety-two natural, existing elements on the earth, our bodies actually only contain eighteen of those elements.

Although the commercial value of these different elements varies from time to time, and people all over the world can sell their organs for thousands of dollars, the actual component elements from which our bodies are made rarely cost a few dollars. In fact scientists found the exact estimate to be...only $5.47 !!

You're probably thinking, "What?! This is unreal! Absurd!" I still marvel at this fact, (this is one of those things like algebra that you're not really supposed to *understand* it, but just *believe* it).

Take a good look at your hand. It is a part of your living body; yet, your hand is made up of "nonliving" atoms. It is only as God places all those atoms together, according to His design for you, that they become "alive". And they will remain alive only as they function in harmony with that great design.

My point in saying all this is not so you will have a lower self esteem, but so we can really stand in awe and marvel at God's creation and remember how truly, without His Spirit living in us, we are as plain and worthless as the dust. It is only by the breath of God that your body has life. Without it, your body would immediately begin to decompose and quickly return to dirt on the ground.

The whole of creation testifies the genius of God's creative hand! Albert Einstein said, "Everyone who is seriously interested in the pursuit of science becomes convinced that a spirit is manifest in the laws of the universe-a spirit vastly superior to man, and one in the face of which our modest powers must feel humble."

As C.S. Lewis perfectly describes it in his book entitled, "Mere Christianity". He says "Of course we never wanted, and never asked, to be made into the sort of creatures He is going to make us into. But the question is not what we intended ourselves to be, but what He intended us to be when He made us. He is the inventor, we are only the machine. He is the painter, we are the picture. How should we know what He means us to be by like? You see, He has already made us into something very different from what we were. Long ago, before we were born, when we were inside our mothers' bodies, we pass through various stages. We were once rather like vegetables, and once rather like fish; it was only at a later stage that we became like human babies. And if we had been conscious at those earlier stages, I dare say we would have been quite contented to stay vegetables or fish, and would not have wanted to be made into babies. But all the time He knew His plan for us and was determined to carry it out. Something the same is now happening at a higher level. We may be contented to remain what we call "ordinary people": but He is determined to carry out a different plan." (p.159)

God spoke history long before it came into being. He can move through time as a man flicks through a history book. One time I saw a poster that said, "I know I'm somebody 'cause God don't make no junk!" And that's the truth! But when we look down upon ourselves and inwardly refuse to accept ourselves just as we are, that's as if we're saying, "God, couldn't you have done a better job when you made me?"

"But now, O Lord, thou art our father; we are the clay; and thou our potter; and we all are the work of thy hand.

You...Fearfully and Wonderfully Made

Shall the thing formed say to him that formed it, why hast thou made me thus?" "Hath not the potter power over the clay...?" —Romans 9:20-21

I remember a few years ago, I was having an "identity crisis" in accepting my height. In my mind I said, "Yes, I totally accept myself" but my actions said something different. What was my problem? I wanted to be shorter. Can you believe that?! At that time my family and I were missionaries living in Guatemala and all the people there are quite short in stature. I'm just about 5'2, but apart form being blond and blue-eyed, I was usually the one standing a head taller out of the crowd. I thought being short was the greatest thing on earth because then you can wear the highest high heels and still get along fine! So as you can imagine I would pray to God to make me shorter although it never really worked. After studying some more on this subject of self-acceptance, I realized that God must have had some good reason for making me the height that I am. So I have come to accept it as a part of my uniqueness!

The prophet Jeremiah also had to learn this important principle, and he recorded in the Bible when "The word of the Lord came to me, saying, "Before I formed you in the womb I knew you, before you were born I set you apart; I appointed you as a prophet to the nations." "Ah, Sovereign Lord, I said, "I do not know how to speak; I am only a child." -Jeremiah 1:4-6

The word here for "child" translated in Hebrew, refers to the period of "infancy up until the twelfth year of age." Can you imagine that Jeremiah was under twelve years old when God first called him to be prophet!

"But the Lord said to me, "Do not say, 'I am only a child.' You must go to everyone I send you to and say whatever I command you. Do not be afraid of them, for I am with you and will rescue you," declares the Lord." (v.1:7)

As he grew older, "The word came to Jeremiah from the

Lord, saying, Arise, and go down to the potters house, and there I will cause you to hear my words. Then I went down to the potters house, and, behold he wrought a work on the wheels.

.And the vessel that he made of clay was marred in the hand of the potter: so he made it again another vessel, as seemed good to the potter to make it.

Then the word of the Lord came to me, saying, O house of Israel, cannot I do with you as this potter? saith the Lord. Behold as the clay is in the hands of a potter's hand, so are ye in mine hand..." —Jeremiah 18:1-6

The worst lump of clay our Potter" has is better than the best the devil has. But we have to remember that we have to stay soft and pliable in our Potters hands, After a lump of clay sets out for a few days, it gets stale and hard and then it crumbles to pieces.

To *renew* something, is to polish it and clean it up make it look better, but to *restore* something is to take apart all the pieces of it and re-make them in the original way they should be. God wants to restore your life, not only renew it. But if you really *do* want to change something in your life and be transformed, put yourself in the Potter's hands, let him twist you and turn you, break you and remake you, into that new vessel, as it seems good to Him. Because you can't put your life in a better place, than in His hands.

God further reminds us in Isaiah 49:15 saying, "Can a mother forget the baby at her breast? And have no compassion on the child she has borne? Though she may forget, I will not forget you! See, I have engraved you on the palms of my hands..."

You are co-creating your future with God! You are an original. Never has there been, and never again will another person on this earth be like you, in any way! You are a one and only. That special destiny that God has planned for you to fulfill, even before you were born, cannot be fulfilled by anyone else...no one else! There is no plan "B"...or C or D!

First Corinthians 1:25-31 says, "For the foolishness of God is wiser than man's wisdom, and the weakness of God is stronger than man's strength. Brothers, think of what you were called. Not many of you were wise by human standards; not many were influential; not many were of noble birth. But God chose the foolish things of this world to shame the wise; God chose the weak things of this world to shame the strong. He chose the lowly things of this world and the despised things, and the things that are not, to nullify the things that are, so that no man may boast before him. It is because of him that you are in Jesus Christ...Let him who boasts, boast in the Lord."

We can see this in many examples in the Bible such as Jacob, a deceiver, but he was called to "father" the Israelite nation (Genesis 27). Joseph, the despised one of his twelve brothers, he became a slave, a prisoner, and yet he saved his family and the whole kingdom of Egypt from starvation (Genesis 39). Moses, a shepherd in exile and a murderer, he had speech problems, but God called him to lead the whole nation Israel out of bondage and into the promise land (Exodus 3). Gideon, a poor, scared farmer, yet God called him to deliver Israel from Midian (Judges 6:11). David, a shepherd boy, and the youngest of his family, yet he became Israel's greatest king (1 Samuel 16). Jephthah, the son of a prostitute, hated by his step brothers, and God called him up to be the leader of the battle where he delivered Israel from the Ammonites (Judges 11:1). Esther, an orphan and a slave girl, through her God-given wisdom, saved her whole country from death and became the next queen of Judah. Peter, a simple fisherman, God called him to be one of his chosen twelve, he became an apostle, a leader of the early church, and a writer of two New Testament letters (Matthew 4:18-20). And in Luke 1:27-38, Mary, a humble peasant girl, yet God chose her to be the mother of Jesus, the son of God, and the list could go on and on! And although in Bible times, he used the poor, the blind, the dumb, the deaf, the prostitute, the leper, the beggar, the cripple, the weak, and just whoever was willing, He still does today! God chooses the foolish and weak things of this world so that when He exalts it, no man can boast.

4

Finding Your Identity in the Midst of a Generation Lost in Space

My parents tell the story of a young girl they knew in Argentina who was born with a crooked nose. She never like it and finally decided to have plastic surgery done to correct it. Years after the operation, she married and her first daughter was born. As her husband took the baby in his arms and gazed into the face of his child, he exclaimed, "Where in the world did she get that nose?!"

Genesis 1:26-27, "Then God said, Let us make man in our image, in our likeness...So God created man in his own image, in the image of God he created him; male and female he created them."

What do you think it means to be "made in the image of God?" In the original Hebrew concordance, this word, *image* means: "a shade, an illusion, a resemblance or a representative figure of something." God created you to be a reflector of Him on this earth that's why he created you in

His "image". God made you as you are, in order to use you as He planned.

In a book entitled "Creation and the Fall" Dietrich Bonhoeffer said, "Man shall proceed from God as His ultimate, his new work, and as the image of God in his creation. There is no transition here from somewhere or other, there is new creation. This has nothing to do with Darwinism: quite independently of this man is the only thing which remains the new, free, unfinished, undetermined work of God. In our concern with the origin and nature of man, it is a hopeless to attempt to make a gigantic leap back into the world of the lost beginning. It is hopeless to want to know for ourselves what man was originally, to identify here man's ideal with the creational reality of God, not to understand that we can know about the man of the beginning only if we start from Christ. Because man differs from the other creatures in that God himself is in him, in that he is God's image in which the free Creator views himself." (p. 36-37)

For over five thousand years, mankind has sought to regain the feeling of security, self-acceptance, and the genuine, unconditional love as it was originally experienced in the Garden. However, none of it seems to work because this is a spiritual problem we are facing, and a spiritual problem can never be solved with any natural solution. Even before the fall of man, God designed a master plan, and our Master Creator is still working from the same blueprint that He began with from the Garden of Eden with Adam and Eve, in the beginning of life. I am convinced that when you truly discover what God initiated in the beginning, then you will understand what He is presently doing today, because God's purpose has never changed!

Have you ever stopped to think that the only aspect of creation that struggles with its identity, is mankind? The birds, bees, dogs and fleas don't give this issue of identity a second thought! And with the exception of mankind, God's

Finding Your Identity

whole creation is at peace with its inherent design and ultimate destiny.

All through this book I really want to stress this point and talk a lot about finding your identity and purpose in life, because we are spiritual, eternal beings confined inside a human experience for this moment of time. What we do with our *spiritual* life is what determines the outcome of our lives and where our soul will spend all of eternity. This generation is a lost generation and all around us we can see the feelings of hopelessness contained within the heart of it. We have sown to the wind and we are reaping the whirlwind. And as long as we keep sowing the seeds of worthlessness in our generation, we will reap the fruit of destruction, and not only upon us but also in the next generation to come, our siblings, future family, and our descendants. So I think it is even more important that we become aware of this and be the ones to change the course of the direction we are going.

In a great book I read, called the "Image Maker" by Terry Crist, he quotes, "It is our blindness to the basic worth of mankind that prevents us from even acknowledging the existence of God. To devalue the creation is to deny the Creator. To devalue the identity of the image bearer is to deny the creatorial right of The Image Maker."

As we already talked about in the first chapter, creation is simply a material conformation to the existence of God. "For since the creation of the world God's invisible qualities-his eternal power and divine nature-have been clearly seen, being understood from what has been made, so that men are without excuse." —Romans 1:20

You will never discover who you were meant to be if you use another person to find yourself. The way we think others perceive us will have a rippling affect on our actions, our self-esteem, and the way we feel about ourselves. Basing our self-worth on what we believe others think of us will cause us to become addicted to their approval. If you want to know who you are, look at God. The key to understanding life is in the source of life, not in the life itself. You are who you are because God took you out of Himself. If you want to know who you are, you must look at the Creator, not the creation.

In fact, the highest form of admiration and worship is imitation. Most of us find it easier to *imitate* than simply *be*. And that's normal. That's why Jesus said to "learn of Me for I am gentle and humble in heart..." —Matthew 11:29

One factor in determining the worth of something is by how much someone is willing to pay for it. And if there is anything I want you to remember out of this whole chapter, it is this: *Jesus gave you your worth with the price he was willing to pay for you. This price is the highest price one has ever paid for something because is was paid for by blood at the cross of Calvary.*

Only as we "live and move and find our being" in Him, will we truly discover whom we were really meant to be, because our identity is clearly linked to His existence. You and I live in a world where our peers label us as who we are and what our worth is, but God's word is the only thing that should give us our identity!

Many times we have been deceived into thinking that "we need to dress and be like, whatever kind of people we want to reach", to win them for Christ. So tell me, do you have to look like a prostitute to reach the prostitutes? Do you have to look and act like a drunkard to reach the drunkards? Do you have to become a drug-addict to reach the drug addicts? No. Jesus did not become like any of these people, yet He reached them all. When we become "like them to reach them" we are communicating the message that, "what you're doing is not wrong, your life-style is *OK*."

We as Christians are supposed to be different in the way we act, dress, and talk. But not just different from the world, but also different from some other Christians. Because the

Finding Your Identity

world doesn't want anymore people who look and act like them, they want people who are outstanding and have answers—that shows visible results—for their society, culture and generation. Sadly many times we let the world know that they have it all, when we pursue after the same things that they seek after. They are supposed to imitate us as we imitate Jesus! *We* have to be the ones to shape the society of our world rather than be influenced by it. Always remember to keep your focus on God, and not compare yourself to anyone. You have to be non-conformist. In other words, be able to live in this culture without being *molded* by this culture. We are to be molded by the Holy Spirit. This issue about "being different" is not just about the clothes you wear. It's not about suddenly going out and dying your hair green or getting dreadlocks and piercings. We are to be chrysalises, not chameleons!

Being different is all about a non-conformity to this secular culture around us. It's about "being in the world but not of it". It's about saying, "God I'll go anywhere you take me, I'll listen and obey anything you say." Being different is not primarily about the outward, although that is a big part of it. It's about the Spirit, that Holy Spirit that is in you.

We don't do this so we'll be better than our friends, but so that we ourselves can be stronger in Jesus Christ. Because you can always find someone who you can say you're better than, but that's not the point. We're not here on this earth to beat them with our standards. Walk alongside them. Love them and help them. It would be difficult if there were only two or three people who wanted to be different that's why we have to do it together. As the body of Christ we need each other. When we make small compromises that lower our testimony, we may still be doing great and have a great ministry but it won't be as effective. Like with a garden hose that has some dirt in it. Water *does* come out easily and it may still get the job done, but it won't be as fast or as effective as if it were totally clear and free from "cloggy" impurities!

Remember you are supposed to be a transparent reflection of the beauty of Jesus himself, when people look at you. You were made in His image and likeness, don't change that image!

5

Restoring the Image

I remember one time, it was a Saturday afternoon and I was trying to clean out all the junk in my closet when I heard a knock at the door. I ran to my window and saw it was my brother's friend who had stopped by to pick up a guitar. There wasn't anyone else at home, so it was up to me to go meet him. These kinds of "visitors" always seemed to come at the wrong time! According to me, I wasn't "perfectly" dressed, so I told him (from my window) that I'd be down in just one second. Then I dived into my closet, pulled out some clothes, changed into them, then ran to my mirror, "quickly" fixed my hair, put on some makeup, and *then* I went down to open the door for him. Poor guy! I can't imagine what he must have been thinking! I kept him waiting so long for nothing, when all he wanted to do was pick up a guitar!

    We girls are all about fashion and appearance so just as a little side note to you girls, 1 Peter 3:4 reminds us about our beauty that, "Instead, it should be that of your inner self, the unfading beauty of a gentle and quiet spirit, which is of great worth in God's sight." What is the best part of a package? The wrapper, or the gift inside? The gift inside!

Think of all the most beautiful, glamorous, and most popular stars, supermodels, and singers. The media paints them like they are the happiest people in the world, right? After all, they *do* have everything they could ever want. But the reality is... they don't have everything they want. You could ask any one of them and if they really told you the truth, deep down in their heart, they're some of the most miserable people around. Even Miss Americas' have problems with low self-esteem!

Remember Proverbs 11:22 warns us, "As a jewel of gold in a swine's snout, so a fair woman which is without discretion."

I've seen plenty of some of the prettiest girls who are as rotten as swine! (not to mention, I used to be one of them). So girls, lets not make that terrible mistake. But as it said in the verse, so is a pretty girl "without discretion." That means that one of the main qualities we need to exercise in our "inner self" is discretion. Discretion is simply taking notice and avoiding words, actions, and attitudes, that could bring about some undesirable consequences.

An eighteen year old guy once told me, "The media rates appearance as all-important, but sincere Christian guys are looking for girls more along the lines of Proverbs 31:30."

Regarding "Beauty Tips", the well known actress, Audrey Hepburn wrote the following. She said, "For attractive lips, speak words of kindness. For lovely eyes, seek out the good in people. For a slim figure, share your food with the hungry. For beautiful hair, let a child run his or her finger through it. For poise, walk with knowledge and you'll never walk alone. People, more than things, have to be restored, renewed, revived, reclaimed, and redeemed; never throw out anybody. The beauty of a woman is not in the clothes she wears, the figure that she carries, or the way that she combs her hair. The beauty of a woman must be seen from her eyes, because that is the doorway of her heart, the place where love resides. The beauty of a woman is not in a facial mole, but true beauty in a woman is reflected in her soul. It is the caring that she lovingly gives, the passion that she shows. The beauty of a woman with passing years, only grows!" So even more than focusing on the outward appearance and things that are unchangeable, why not focus on the things we *can* change!

Back to you guys...One time my Dad was talking with an ambassador from Colombia.

This ambassador had lost his gloves and was worried because it was part of his military uniform and he had a meeting to attend in a little while. So right away he and my dad started on a search for the mystery of the missing gloves. It was getting closer and closer to the time for him to be leaving for this meeting and by now he was desperately searching for those gloves! My dad had a pair of gloves, that were almost identical to the missing ones, and he offered them since they still couldn't find the others. The ambassador politely refused them because they weren't the exact matching color to his military uniform. So finally, they just set out to find a nice mall and bought a very nice looking pair of gloves, which were the same color of his old ones. An ambassador to another place has to be very careful about every aspect in his appearance, in the same way Christ wants us to be as *His* ambassadors.

In his second letter to the Corinthians, Paul reminds us that "We are therefore Christ's ambassadors, as though God were making his appeal through us..." Since you and I are ambassadors from Heaven, and our mission is to reconnect the world to Him, then I think we should first study about some qualities of ambassadors here on earth.

One quality I found an ambassador here on earth has to have is the willingness to go anywhere his government sends him. He will also enjoy the guaranteed protection of his government only as he stays under their authority. Just as an ambassador maintains constant communication with the government he is representing, we are to maintain that same daily, intense, and constant communication (through prayer) with the president of the Heavenly government we are representing.

When an ambassador goes to another country, he is not subject to the laws of that nation. He can park his car anywhere he wants! He doesn't have to conform to the rules of that society, because he has "diplomatic immunity." You and I also have "diplomatic immunity" because we're no longer under the law of sin and death. We live in a secular, anti-God world and we can't conform to the secular rules and philosophies of this world. You are under Heaven's laws, you're under Heaven's power, and you are a diplomat of Heaven!

My family and I have traveled to many different countries and as good ambassadors we have had to learn to adjust to every country's culture. One of these adjustments came when we moved from Guatemala (my birthplace) to Mexico. A friend and I were working on balloon arrangements for a wedding reception that was going to take place later on that afternoon. At one point an intense gush of wind blew into the building and the balloons started to pop. I told this to my friend and she turned around, looked at them and then looked at me in disbelief and started laughing! You see, the Guatemalan word for "balloon", is the word for "womb" in Mexico. So I was really saying, "The wombs are popping!"

On another occasion a short time after we had moved, I was talking to some friends at the youth group and I heard them say something like, "Oh he took a bath!" and another said, "Well she did too!" I thought, "Bath? Who took a bath and why are they talking about this?!" I'm so glad I didn't voice my thoughts because I later learned that they use that expression for saying, "You messed up" or "I can't believe she did that". Spanish is Spanish, but expressions vary from country to country!

"And they admitted that they were aliens and strangers on earth...they were longing for a better country, a heavenly one. Therefore God is not ashamed to be called their God, for he has prepared a city for them." -Hebrews 11:13,16

As members of the body of Christ, we are here in this world with the mission of representing Jesus to our generation. The word "re-present" literally means "to present the same thing once again". This "representation" actually goes farther than simply acting on His behalf. It involves presenting Jesus to contemporary society in just the same way that He was presented to Israel during His earthly life and ministry. As an ambassador of the Kingdom, you are to represent Him to those who are around you. That's why Paul called us "living epistles' seen and read by all men."

What do you think all your unsaved friends, co-workers, and classmates think about when they hear your name? Have you been a "Jesus with skin on" to them? We have to keep reminding ourselves of this. The radical nature of being an everyday Christian is that you present your body as a "living sacrifice", refusing to be conformed to the spirit of this world, as you renew your mind to God's perfect will for your life. A good ambassador is he who seeks to represent his Lord with dignity and honor. Are you doing this?

"But you are a chosen people, a royal priesthood, a holy nation, a people belonging to God, that you may declare the praises of him who called you..." —1 Peter 2:9

I am convinced that if this generation is going to come to faith in the living, true God of the Bible, then it will be because they see modern men and women, guys and girls, living in His presence, twenty-four hours a day, seven days a week, 365 days a year, under His Kingdom's rule.

In the Medieval culture around the 1300's, knights often wore closed helmets that shielded their face, to protect them during times of war, and because of it, it was hard to distinguish friends from foes in the midst of battle. So for identification, each noble family had its own heraldry, which were certain colorful and unique symbols, emblems, and designs displayed on their armor, shields, and banners. People could learn a lot about a man's family background by his coat of arms, which was their family's display of heraldry.

They represented their banner and their banner represented them. When they would go out to battle, they wouldn't hold their flag up to their own army, but to the enemy.

Isaiah 59:19 says that, "When the enemy shall come in like a flood, the Lord shall lift up a standard against him." We have to raise our standards so that we can stand against the enemy and it won't be a question to the world if we're a Christian or not. Guys and girls, it has to show! To be radical and set apart from the world is to have a fear of the Lord, not a fear of man. I am more and more convinced that if we are (and I know we are) the "generation upon whom the ends of the world are to come", then it is even more important that we come to realize who we are in Christ and the purpose for which we live.

One summer, some friends of mine went to Disneyland, California. They told me that underground in the park, there is a whole network of costumes, paints, and other things that are used for all the rides and shows there. On every door of the underground before going out, there is a sign that reads, "You are now walking on stage".

This is a short sentence but with a great meaning behind it. We have to remember for our own life that every day, from the time you step out of your room in the morning, you are walking on stage as an ambassador representing Jesus Christ.

Sadly, there are no dress rehearsals for life; we are on the stage right away. Even when we have made many mistakes in the past, it is possible to place our lives completely in His hands, to make something great and beautiful out of that design He started. That which had been "messed up", is now made new! God created you with a purpose and a destiny, you will never find true satisfaction in life until you do find it. So don't let anything or anyone, cause you to miss it!

As long as you look around and wish you had another person's hair, clothes, personality or popularity, you will be the most miserable person that walked the face of this planet! But when you start to see yourself as God sees you- something beautiful and perfectly made, created with a great purpose and destiny, then no matter what the circumstances, you will be the happiest person on earth!

6

God Wants Me to Do... What With My Life???

"Where did you come from? Why are you here? Where are you going? What is your purpose for living in this life?"

Before writing this chapter I asked these questions to many Christian teens. Surprisingly, after thinking about it a while they would answer, "Good question, I had never thought about that. Well, I really don't know." This is supposed to be one of the things that differs Christians from the world is that we know where we came from and we know where we're going! We have purpose and direction in life!

To think that God created you for a specific job to do in this generation is an intriguing thought. How seriously do you go about finding this purpose? Do you just stumble upon it and look back in retrospect and see that you somehow found your life's purpose? Or do you actively seek out the purpose that God has prepared for you?

Take a minute to think about this: everyone does everything with a purpose. It's a universal fact. We eat food because we want to live. We play sports to stay healthy. We take showers to keep clean. We go to school to learn. We work to make money...or some people steal and kill to get money. Some people take drugs to get "high." People drink and smoke to forget their problems. Whether it's a good purpose or a bad one, *everyone does everything with a purpose!* No man will build a big, huge, beautiful mansion and then tell his fellow worker, "Now, what was it we were we going to do with this? Why did we even make it in the first place?"

So when it comes to *our* purpose in life, God didn't just create you and then say, "Well, now what should I do with him/her?" Do you get what I am saying?

The simple act that you are alive today means that God created you for a special, unique purpose. Everyone who ever lived and everyone who will live, was created by God to live in this world for a special purpose.

Someone said there are three kinds of people in the world-those who make things happen, those who watch them happen, and those who never knew that anything at all was happening. Which one are you? If you don't have a vision for your life, you will be like many other Christians today who come to the end of their life still wandering around, clueless, nameless, and aimlessly on this earth. They still don't have any sense of direction in life or an answer for these questions.

And there are a zillion ways you can find your life calling. The next ones that I name are just a few to get you started. Your life *calling* can be temporal, or for life, it just depends on where you feel the Lord leads you.

Find something you can do well for God, and then spend your time, energy and life doing it because it will count for Eternity. For me it was reading and writing and that's what led me to write this book you are now reading. One thing I

God Wants Me to Do...What With My Life???

do want to say is that serving has its place in every person's life calling and life purpose, because serving is one of God's attributes. I heard a pastor once say the best way to know if you have a servant's heart is to see how you respond to a servants' jobs.

God's opportunities for us are endless, it is just up to us to find what your life calling is. When you come to the end of your life what do you want to look back on?

Just as any machine will mess up when it isn't working as it should. In the same way, when we are not working as we should, when your machine is not functioning as it's designer (God) created it to be and do, then you're going to be the most miserable! Absolutely miserable! And it gets to the point where you feel like, "Hey, I'm tired of this life. I just wasn't created for this." Because you're missing the mark!

David Livingston was a doctor born in Scotland. His purpose in fulfilling God's plan was to go to Africa and share with the people there a message of hope and salvation. It was in Africa where he died. At his death the natives gently removed his heart and buried it in the Africa he so dearly loved. As his body was carried through the streets of London to the final resting place of Westminster Abbey, one man wept openly. A friend gently consoled him, asking if he had known Livingston as a personal friend. "I weep not for Livingston but for myself," the first man said, adding, "he lived and died for something, but I have lived for nothing."

What do you live for? What are you willing to die for? Think of your life in terms of sixty years from now, what do you want to have accomplished? What do you think God wants you to have accomplished before you go home?

Your *ultimate goal* in life is to be a soul-winner because that is the only thing that will count for Eternity. So your life calling includes the group of people whom God wants you to give the life-changing love and truth.

7

The Great Go-Mission

Nine Tips to Accomplishing the Unfinished Task of World Evangelism

I once heard a true story of a man who went into a Christians book store, and asked, "May I see your evangelism section please? The attendant asked, "What's evangelism?"

Sometimes I think the disciples of Jesus we a lot like me—a bit slow when it comes to catching the obvious. There were volumes of things that Jesus told them straight away that they just didn't get. Maybe that's why Jesus waited until the very end to give them their most important assignment of all. It was the one thing He didn't want them to forget. So He gathered them together before He went back to Heaven and told them in the simplest terms possible, "Go into all the world and preach the good news to all creation." —Mark 16:15

Charles Finney said, "It is the greatest business of every Christians to win souls."As soon as you give your heart to

Jesus, and make Him the Lord of your life, you definitely have something to give the world, and we actually "owe" something to everyone who has not yet heard about Jesus Christ and the sacrifice He made for them on the cross. The gift of salvation is like something that is to be reproduced, multiplied and given out to as many as possible. As we have freely received, we are to freely give. We are *all* commissioned to preach Jesus, make disciples, genuinely love one another, and humbly serve the world. And the best part is you don't have to wait to some how be "officially anointed" and go out to minister to others. You have been anointed since the day you gave your life to Jesus, and your time is now! God is just waiting for you to get moving! Bloom where you're planted!

1. Realize Your Time Is Now

"Wherefore he saith, Awake thou that sleepest, and arise from the dead, and Christ shall give thee light. See then that ye walk circumspectly, not as fools, but as wise, redeeming the time, because the days are evil. Wherefore be ye not unwise, but understanding what the will of the Lord is. " — Ephesians 5:14-17

A young girl once told me about a dream she had about Hell. She saw Satan sitting on his throne, looking for a demon to send to earth. He called one demon and asked him, "Do you want to go to the earth for me to deceive people and destroy some souls?" "Sure, I'll go." he replied. "And what will you tell the people?" Satan asked. "I'll tell them that there is *no* God, and that everything other people say about religion is all a crazy myth." he answered. Satan said, "No that won't work, you can't go anymore, because things won't go well with you."

Then Satan asked another demon and he said, "I'll go,

The Great Go-Mission

I'll tell them that there *is* a kind and merciful God, but it's a ridiculous, stupidity to serve Him." Satan responded, "No, don't go, you won't have success either."

Yet a third demon offered to go and Satan asked him what he would say, and the demon replied, "I'll tell them that there *is* a God, full of love and mercy. I'll tell them, that Jesus lived and died for their sins on the cross, and that his resurrection is all true. I'll tell them that they need to get their lives straight with God and read the Bible. But then I will tell them that *there is still time.*"

"Go," Satan said, "you will have success." That demon did come to earth and has had very much success. He has even been whispering those same words in our ears: "You don't need to pray so much, *there is still time*, You don't need to be so committed to serve God now, wait until you're older, *there is still time*, you don't need to forgive yet, wait until you feel like it, *there is still time.* You know you're wrong but you don't need to make things right yet, *there is still time.* You can wait until later to evangelize and win souls, wait until tomorrow to tell that old friend or relative about Jesus, *there is still time."* The biggest lie of the devil, you could ever believe is, that there is still time. But reality is, we are running out of time.

There have been many times in history where Christians and the body of Christ as a whole, was not ready and prepared to wake up and take action to bring in the harvest. Let me tell you of two occasions.

On September 2, 1945, after World War 2, General Douglas McArthur became the military governor of Japan. He influenced sweeping changes in Japan's economic, political, and social life, but he realized that more than anything else, Japan's pressing need was evangelization. With all the pain and poverty that war had brought upon their land, the doors swung wide open for the gospel. General McArthur issued a call to all the missionary societies from every denomination across America. He said, "I told visiting Christian ministers of the need of their work here in Japan. The more missionaries we can bring out here, and the more occupation troops we can send home the better." But sadly, they were not ready and prepared and they said, "We can't, we don't have missionaries because we are committed to China and other countries for now." McArthur pleaded with them saying, "But this is the time for Japan! Japan is open now, and we need missionaries!" But they answered, "We're sorry, we can't."

As a result, thousands of Chinese souls died without Jesus. Because Christians were not ready and willing to give up their pleasures and lay down their lives for the salvation of others.

In Russia in the summer of 1988, Soviet Premier Mikhail Gorbachev suddenly announced a dramatic change of the Communist policy. The Communists developed a plan known as the "Perestroika" to rebuild its economic and political system on a democratic, free enterprise model. They also adopted a foreign policy known as "Glasnost" which means "openness", claiming that they wanted world peace and had no more plans of conquest. Communism was defeated, opening many new doors for the gospel and evangelization to the Russia people. Can you guess who took the advantage to be the first to go in? The "Playboy" magazine. Tons of pornographic material was shipped into that country and given out free of charge so that the people could receive it and then become addicted. It wasn't tons of Bibles, it was tons of destructive pornographic magazines, because once again Christians were not alert, ready, and prepared to be salt and light, at a time in history when it was so needed.

Early one morning I got up and read the Internet news. It said that 150 youth and children from Australia had died, burned in a cable car because they couldn't get out when, unexpectedly, the cable snapped and burst into fiery flames.

The Great Go-Mission

They were going up the mountain to spend the day skiing.

My heart ached as I thought to myself, "Were they ready to go into Eternity? Did they have a chance to get to know You? Did they have friends that could have told them about Jesus, and didn't?" Then I thought to myself, "And what was I doing during those hours in the morning, that very same day?" It was a Saturday I remembered, so I was probably sleeping in late. Here I was all nice and cuddly in my bed and little did I know that on the other side of the world, there were 150 youth and children stepping into Eternity, maybe without Jesus.

There is a poem I once read and I don't know who wrote it because it just said "Anonymous", but I want its powerful message to challenge your heart. The words are from a lost sinner talking to a Christian when they've both reached eternity.

"My friend, I stand in judgment now, and feel that you're to blame somehow. On earth I walked with you by day, and never did you show the way. You knew the Savior in truth and glory, but never did you tell the story. My knowledge then was very dim, you could have led me safe to Him. And though we lived together, here on earth, you never told me of the second birth. And now I stand before eternal Hell, because of Heaven's glory you did not tell!"

My dear reader, the Christian life is so much more than just getting saved, going to church and living a good life. It's about reaching out to change your generation for Christ!

There are so many hurting people out there, you just can't afford to be one of them. In every battle that has ever been fought, there has always been more wounded, than doctors to care for them, and as a result many have died. In this spiritual battle we are fighting, we cannot stand by and watch men and women, guys and girls, die and go into eternity, in a lake of fire with constant torment, and their blood be upon us...because we kept silent. Witnessing has never been so easy, even today many believers face death and still share God's word. And compared to that, we hold back because someone might laugh! True love must reach out. True love cannot sit on a pew and watch others go to Hell!

Hudson Taylor, the great missionary to China, once said, "It is possible to sing, 'My all is on the altar', and yet be unprepared to sacrifice a ring from one's finger or a picture from one's wall, or a child from one's family, for the salvation of the heathen."

I was once at a church meeting where the preacher asked all those "who had the call to evangelize" to come forward to be prayed for. About one-fourth of the church went forward. My dear reader, *we are ALL called to evangelize!* Because if you are striving to become more like Jesus, His whole goal in life was to "seek and save the lost!"

What would you think of someone who could sit and read a book, while a little child is drowning next to them. What a heart of stone! I mean, what person could just sit there and say, "No, he's not my child. I don't have anything to do with him."

We are guilty of the very same thing! I don't see how any Christian can sit back and feed on God's word, and enjoy the abundant life, while thousands of people are swallowed by death every twenty-four hours!

Sadly, that's just what we've done. As Oswald J. Smith said, "Oh my friends, we are loaded down with countless church activities, while the real work of the Church, that of evangelizing and winning the lost is almost entirely neglected."

I can tell you that 70 to 80 percent of today's evangelical, fundamental, Bible believing church, sits very comfortably in the lukewarm bracket.

Richard Wurmbrand, a Romanian pastor who suffered 14 years of brutal torture for Christ under the reign of communism said, "In the first days after my conversion, I felt that I would not be able to live any longer. Walking on the street, I felt physical pain for every man and woman who passed by. It was like a knife in my heart, so burning was the question of whether or not he or she was saved."

So the first and main step in evangelism is to *get a burden for the lost!*

Mark 16:15 talks about The Great Commission, not The Great *Suggestion.* God's love isn't passive! And if you don't have enough love in your heart to pull your neighbor from the very fires of Hell, then how can you call yourself a Christian? Because my Bible says that "he that loves not, knows not, for God is love."

Religion is when people try to reach God in their own efforts. In the East people lay on beds of nails, and in the West people sit on hard pews, but both things are of equal pain to God's heart! If you are a sleeping saint, Satan will gladly rock your cradle. Guys and girls, the fear of God is lacking in His church and apathy pervades it worldwide!

We have defused our evangelism of its urgency, but we need to get desperate and save this generation before its too late!

2. Staggering Statistics

I don't really like fishing, but I *love* fishing for men! So since we are called to be "fishers of men", I think it is important for us to learn about the skills of a good fisherman, that could relate to soul winning. The first one of these is to *know where the fish are.* Many of us have an overall picture of the need in the world for Jesus, but many times we don't realize just how much.

I studied up the following statistics from the Global Evangelization and the International Bible Society, Barnett and Johnson, A.D. 2000, Global Monitor October '94.

Quoted in context of "The New Context of World Mission" by Bryant L. Myers '96 and Johnstone "Operation World" '93.

We all know that the 10/40 Window-spanning from North Africa to the eastern edge of Asia-is the least evangelized part of the world.

Eighty-six percent of all people groups live in the 10/40 Window, less than two percent of which are Christians. In this needy region:

One billion people have little chance to even hear the gospel unless someone specifically goes there to tell them.

Eighty-five percent of the world's poorest countries are within the un-evangelized world. Of the 925 million absolute poor in the world, 23 percent are Christians.

There are 190 nations in the world, 12,500 ethnic "people groups", and the current global population is around 6 billion.

There are still more than 1,700 people groups in the world who have never heard the gospel.

Between 800 million and 1.3 billion people have never had one single opportunity to respond to the gospel.

Most Christians allocate only 1.2 percent of their missions funding and foreign missionaries to only 1.1 billion of the people who live in the un-evangelized world.

The New Testament is available in a little over 900 languages but...there are 6,528 languages in the world—and 1.1 billion people are illiterate.

Only 1 percent of Bible distribution and only 3 percent of Bible translations are directed toward the least evangelized parts of the world.

There is an average number of 8 Bibles in an American Christian home, and the average amount of money Christians give strictly to mission work per year is...five dollars!

An average of 365,000 babies are born every day, and

The Great Go-Mission

about 147,000 people die every day, and at least thirty-eight percent of these, have never heard!

And meanwhile, evangelical believers all across America spend four times as much money each year on weight-loss programs as they do in spreading the gospel!

Some statistics say that around 51 percent of all the people on the earth are under the age of twenty-five. And 95 percent of all people in general get saved *before* the age of 25. So I'm thinking, if we realize that salvation comes mainly before the age of twenty-five, why aren't we taking more time and effort investing in the lives of youth?!

Some statistics also say that 80 percent of all youth were in church one generation ago, today 12 percent are in church and only 3 percent of that 12 percent are really born again and on fire for Christ. So literally speaking, we've lost 90 percent of the youth of America to the world! We're in big trouble! This is the future church!

This prospect of evangelism seems totally overwhelming to most of us, I think it may be the reason why many people just set this very important area of the Christian life aside. When we consider the current population of the world, we see this task as impossible! Well, I got some great news...it *is* possible!

I studied some different resources about global evangelism and was so astonished by what I found, and I am so excited to be able share these facts with you.

A human pole count of world population, which was in taken in the year 2000 revealed that there are about 6 billion people in the whole world. The question is, how long would it take to evangelize the whole world if *you* led just one person to Christ each day, and each one of those people did the same? Hard question! In other words, today I win one, tomorrow we each win one, the next day each one of us wins one, and it keep on and on. (We are also imagining that each one of those people received Christ right away and set out do the same, and got the same results.) I guessed probably about thirty years. After checking this out with some global evangelism organizations, I still didn't believe it, so I also multiplied this all up (a task, which took me quite a long time to do!) OK, are you ready for this…I found out…?

It would take only 33 days. That's only a little over one month! You're probably thinking, "Whhaaat?! Are you sure you got that right?! How can this be?" My only logical explanation is that we humans are as ants on this planet called earth, and we tend to magnify things a little bigger than what they really are! Based on this number of humans on this earth, here is another incredible fact I found out. Did you know that if the whole world's population, from every tribe and tongue, were gathered together, standing side by side, shoulder to shoulder, they would all fit in the state of Florida alone! And to think that we are scared of over populating the world! Actually I think this planet's a little empty, don't you think? Yes, we are always seeing pictures of places like China overly crowded with people. But hey, you could probably go downtown in any big city and take a picture where there are crowds of people and get the same results! And there are countries in the world where people are "crowded" but because they don't spread out! (And that's when God brings persecution to a nation, because He said to "go into all the world!").

Matthew 5:13 says, "Ye are the salt of the earth…" That word "salt" translated in the original Greek actually means *prudence*. We as Christians are the "prudence" of the earth.

We are supposed to be stopping the world from "going bad!" But it takes boldness! I know that there are already enough Christians in the whole world today to accomplish the unfinished task of world evangelism. I want you to know that the job can be done. Christ will never, and has never asked us to do something that He knows we will not be able to accomplish. If us as Christians would just do our part, and

The Great Go-Mission

be salt *and* light to a lost and dying world, it could be done!

I once heard on the radio an interview with a guy about what he thought about Hell and being left behind when Jesus comes back. He replied, "Oh me? I'm not going to be left behind, I'm going to Heaven too." Then they asked him, "And how have you come to that conclusion?" He said, "Oh, uh...just because He'll want me up there too I guess!"

Statistics show that while most people believe in Heaven and think and hope to go there when they die, they don't believe that Hell is real. People can't imagine how such a merciful God would allow anyone to spend eternity in a place of "utter darkness" and "Eternal torment", so they dismissed it as a myth. Hell *is* real!!

But if we were *really* convinced that every person whose name is not written in the Lamb's Book of Life is headed for Hell, wouldn't we be more aggressive in our efforts to save them?

Years ago, there was a really good Christian song that came out called, "Asleep in the Light" from Keith Green's album, "No Compromise". I want you to hear its words, let them sink into your heart, and catch the spirit of what it's saying.

"Do you see, do you see all the people sinking down? Don't you care, don't you care, are you going to let them drown? How can you be so numb not to care if they come, you can close your eyes and pretend the job's done.

Bless me Lord, bless me Lord, you know that's all I ever hear. No one aches, no one hurts, no one even sheds one tear. Open up, open up and give yourself away, you see the need, you hear the cry, so how can you delay?

God's calling and you're the one, but like Jonah you run. He's told you to speak but you keep holding it in, oh can't you see its such a sin..."

I pray that God will give you an even greater burden and a stronger passion for the precious souls of the people who are sliding into darkness without Jesus—whether they live on the other side of the world or right next door.

3. Be Bold

"How then can they call on one they have not believed in? And how can they believe in the one of whom they have not heard? And how can they hear without someone preaching to them?" —Romans 10:14

Have you ever had that weird feeling inside when you witness to certain people? One of the greatest things that keeps most of us from being bolder and bravely proclaiming the gospel, is the fear of man and the fear of rejection.

I know each one of us could probably come up with over ten million excuses not to witness, and if anyone in the world should have the boldness and qualifications to speak, I think it would be Paul. In 1 Corinthians 2:1-3 Paul says, "And I, brethren, when I came to you, came not with excellency of speech or of wisdom, declaring unto you the testimony of God...and I was with you in weakness, and in fear, and in much trembling."

In the third verse here, Paul tells us how he was feeling and I am convinced that every person who wants to be a witness for Christ should have these four qualifications for witnessing. Number 1. You should not have excellency in speech, 2. You should have weakness, 3. You should have fear and 4. You should have *much* trembling. Now, do you qualify?

Then he gives us the key in verse two where he says, "For I am determined not to know anything among you, save Jesus Christ, and him crucified." Paul was a man who loved the Truth and he loved sinners enough to preach God's Truth to them.

A very wise man once said, "An act of courage isn't

The Great Go-Mission

necessarily done by those who feel brave when they do it. True courage is he who feels fear and yet does it anyway. Courage isn't the absence of fear, but the conquering of it."

One summer, my family and some friends decided we would go to Six Flags. We just *had* to try out their newest new roller coaster, "Mr. Freeze". If you've been on it, you know that this roller coaster does a complete 360-degrees loop, goes up vertically, and then does the loop again backwards! I know that will seem like nothing in a few years, but for us this was a mega-monster! After waiting in line for about two hours, I started to question whether or not I really wanted to do this. But I "gave into peer-pressure" (not a good thing to do!) and now I *love* roller coasters! Because the more you experience the ride, the less fearful you become. But did you know that between 1973 and 1996, there were 45 deaths and over 6,000 injuries in America from roller coaster-type rides.

Think of it. We are prepared to put our lives on the line- to "risk death", for the *love* of fear. But for the *fear* of fear, we are prepared to let sinners go to Hell forever. What then is the difference between the two fears? One we love, one we hate. One is a thrill, the other a torment. The tormenting fear we feel is very *real*, yet the reason for it is irrational. Let me show you why.

One time I was listening to a preacher on a tape (well I really wasn't listening!) but then I heard something that caught my attention and challenged the life into me. The man asked the question, "If you were going to be given one thousand dollars for every person you witnessed to, would you be more zealous in your evangelism?"

I thought, "Yes! For a thousand dollars? Yes! I think I would!" Then the normal scenario is this: I'll be sitting on a plane, ridding a bus, or something like that, with someone beside me, and I'll be trying to trick my own brain (as I always do when trying to witness) into thinking that these are the last minutes on earth for me and for that person, and I'm trying to save him from an eternity in Hell. And I'm arguing with myself, "Ok, I think I'll start out by saying...no, no Cristina that might offend them. Hmmm, yeah, I think I'll say...no then they'll think..." And it goes on and on!

But if I was going to get one thousand dollars for every person I witnesses to... then I'd probably just shout, "Hey! You over there! Where do you want to spend Eternity, Heaven or Hell?! Don't sleep while I'm trying to talk to you!" Then I'd probably grab the phone book and be dialing all the numbers in it. Next I'd probably send an email forward to everyone I could get a hold of saying, "Hi! My name is Cristina, I'm a seventeen year old Jesus freak and I want to tell you...(and then I'd go through my whole sermon on the plan of salvation!), then I would end this email forward, (like those types we all hate) saying, "so if you want to be safe from Hell's flames on Judgment day, forward this to at least one hundred people (remember I'm getting one thousand dollars for each one of these who forwards it!). The death sentence for violating God's Law is the standard for judgment on Judgment Day. You can choose to delete this and ignore God's offer of mercy and but if you pass through the door of death without the Savior, you will have to face the Holy and just God whose law you have violated. God Bless."

I had to examine my own heart and say, "Would I be more passionate and zealous for money, than I would be for God?"

Now let me challenge you with this thought, "Could you deal with your 'fear-of-man-problem' for the love of money, when you can't deal with it for the love of God?"

One of the greatest things I have most asked of God is that He make me bold, and often when I'm scared and nervous trying to witness to someone, I'll just think of this and

I'll say, "God I know I would do it for money, I know I would. So how much more for You."

You can be sure that if God can use a young, scared, female, freighty-cat like me, then He can use any man or woman on the face of this planet, who will only ask and believe.

Second Corinthians 2:15-17 says that, "…we are to God the aroma of Christ among those who are being saved and those who are perishing. To the one we are the smell of death; to the other, the fragrance of life. And who is equal to such a task? Unlike so many, we do not peddle the word of God for profit. On the contrary, in Christ we speak before God with sincerity, like men sent from God."

Of all the people on earth who should be able to fearlessly look the world in the eye, it is Christians, because we are speaking the Gospel of truth. In other words, we are not selling anything. All we are "after" is the Eternal well being of others. So really you have nothing to loose! If you present someone with the gospel and they reject it, you have not lost anything. If you present them with the gospel and they receive it…then you've gained the whole world! Don't get down in the dumps when someone laughs, mocks, and rejects you.

If you're doing it the right way, people *will* reject you! But you can still keep on being one happy Christian! A candle looses nothing in *trying* to light another candle!

The most important, worthwhile, Eternal, thing you could ever do in your life and especially as a youth, is to be a soul winner. Thomas Jefferson said, "The fortune of our lives…depends on employing well, the short period of youth." Remember, you may be the *only* Christian your peers will ever see or rub shoulders with in their whole entire life.

In any church you go to, you'll find that 95 percent of the all people came to Christ through a friend or family member. Does this tell us something? Your friends and all those around you, taste Christ through you. Others will know if they want anything to do with God according to how much they see Jesus himself reflected through you. It is up to us to be that sweet savor of the gospel. It is up to you and me to show the world the difference that only Jesus makes in a person's life, not just that we aren't boring, hypocritical "church-goers," but that we actually have something they don't have and that they are totally missing out on the very essence and meaning of life itself!

Charles Spurgeon said, "Brethren, do some something, do something, do something! While societies and unions make constitutions, let us win souls. I pray you, be men of action all of you…our one aim I to win souls; and this we are not to talk about, but do in the power of God!"

4. Be Passionate!

If you ask the average non-Christian, un-churched person what he thinks God is like, you would probably get some pretty colorful answers! If you asked him what he thought Christians were like, a "nicer" reply would probably be, "boring!" To some people we tell about Jesus, it's almost like we are telling them, "Give your life to some huge Unknown Being and join the most boring club in the world!"

Christianity is never boring. Read the books of Hebrews and Acts and you'll see that life for these passionate Christians was anything but boring. These heroes of faith were thrown into fiery furnaces, lion's cages, shipwrecked, beaten, tortured, chained, stoned, mocked, and flogged. So if you're a boring Christian, that's *your* fault!

Make yourself passionate! Get excited about the things of God! We can't reclaim this generation for Christ if all we have to offer is an empty, shallow religiosity others have seen in the past. We must have the passionate, vibrant, zealous, New Testament faith that offers relevant answers to the un-churched masses of people that are starved for reality! How can we say that this "Jesus stuff" really works when all we do is we act like a bunch of loners or losers? They are more likely to answer, "No thanks, I think I'll try another beer."

Guys and girls, if our lives fail to reflect the quality of life He offers us, then we are just like those advertisers we see on TV selling a product we know he himself doesn't really even use! That is quite hard to do because your life is the living presentation. Passion is lacking!

On the radio there are many Christians airing their programs, but on there I have heard some of the dullest preachers in my life! Right on the radio!

Our English word, "enthusiasm" comes from two Greek words, *en* and *theos* meaning "in God". If you're in God and God is in you, then there should be an enthusiasm in your heart abut sharing the gospel!

Society is attracted to passionate people because passionate people are contagious! Have you ever wondered why sports stadiums are always so full? I've even seen some people who don't especially like sports or really even understand the game itself, but they are sure to go to sport stadiums. Why? Because the stadiums are always overflowing with passionate people! It's always so fun, exciting, and energizing to be around passionate people! In the same way, we are like the "bait" for what God wants to do, and live bait sure works better than dead bait!

Christianity is the only religion in the world that brings fulfillment in life because it's something that's alive, because it is the Holy Spirit that is breathing into it! Christianity is not boring, untrue or irrelevant; it's all about living life to the full! Just as salt brings out the flavor in food, we as Christians are to "bring out the flavor" and real meaning of life!

5. Discover His Methods

"I'm going out to fish," Simon Peter told them, and they said, "We'll go with you." So they went out and got into the boat, but that night they caught nothing. Early in the morning, Jesus stood on the shore...He called out to them, "Friends, haven't you any fish?" "No," they answered. He said, "Throw your net on the right side of the boat
and you will find some." When they did, they were unable to haul the net in because of the large number of fish." -John 21: 3-6 (NIV)

Many, if not most times, God's methods are not what we expect, because his thoughts are higher than ours. That's why you have to listen closely to the heart of God and seek his direction all the time.

I remember one summer afternoon I went out with a team to do evangelism in the local town square. We gathered a small crowd and began to witness, when suddenly I heard a loud, rambling noise behind me. And it wasn't the rapture either! It was this drunk guy standing there yelling at us, "What do you think you #$%^&* fools are doing?!" as he waved his bottle of whiskey at us. Praise God for him! He was perfect bait. As many crowds of people flocked to see what all the fuss was about, he just helped double our crowd. So never fear hecklers! God may very well send them your way to give you a hand in drawing a crowd.

There was another recent story I got off the Internet about a tribe in Papua New Guinea. There were some missionaries who had gone to Papua New Guinea as missionaries and win the people to Christ. Amid all their efforts, everything they tried to do to relate to these tribal people seemed to be in vain. Discouraged but determined not to give up, they gave it all they could to accomplish the task they had set out to do. One day, one of the missionaries was preaching from the Bible story in John Chapter 9 where Jesus spat on the ground, made mud, and then took the mud, placed it on the blind man's eyes and healed him. After that short story, all the tribesmen started getting excited and wanted to know more about this Jesus.

The reason was, the missionaries later found out, that as a tradition of the tribesmen, the tribesmen would gather all the men of the village together and have a spitting contest. The man who could spit the farthest, won the contest, and became the ruling, highest chief of that village. So at hearing this Bible story, all the tribesmen exclaimed, "This Jesus they are telling us about, He must be the Greatest Chief and He even has power in his spit!"

Many times I think people reject the gospel because of the way we present it. We are commanded to go and "teach all nations". Webster's definition of the word "Teach" is: "To instruct, inform, and communicate to another the knowledge of that of which he was before ignorant."

In other words, to tell it to him in a way that he will understand. We don't realize this but many times we are speaking such a "religious" language that other people don't have a clue as to what we're talking about or what we mean. If we expect to get a message across and reach the unreached, then we have to be aware of the importance of this! Charles Spurgeon said, "A preacher who will not condescend to the use of anecdotes, will remain forever a river of ice flowing upon his congregation." That's why Jesus spoke so much in parables, because they were practical stories people could relate to and understand. It's all about communicating Biblical truth to a secular audience in a way that they understand.

We are not trying to change their religion, we're trying

to make Jesus real for them. We want them to discover Christ for themselves. You want the light to turn on in their own heads, not that they believe it just because you told them. Because when you discover something for yourself, chances are you will remember it for a lifetime.

One time I along with some other friends were invited to go meet and talk to some gang members from a dark ghetto area of the city in which we lived. We went to Punkville and I had such a great time talking to those gangsters and just taking the time to hear them pour out their hearts to us. But as I sat amid the filth, foul language, drugs, rock music, and alcohol, I thought, "This is it! This is how you reach a generation!" Jesus was the friend of sinners! He spent 90 percent of his time, life and ministry with them! It was the Pharisees who hated Jesus for that. Holiness is not separation from *sinners*, but from *sin*. Like Jesus we should be a friend of sinners, yet remain untainted by the things of this world.

George Stewart said, "The Church after all is not a club of saints; it is a hospital for sinners." If you care about anyone in this world, you won't be sitting in a "holy click!" We are just being light where there's light, and salt among salt, but what good is salt if it's out of the shaker? Where is our compassion?! I cannot imagine anyone who could call himself a Christian, but not have a burning passion for the lost! Get out of *your* comfort zone and get into theirs.

So many people today have been "pushed" out of church because they didn't "fit" in with the "pretty-perfect-picture" of a church's "normal" Christian. It's almost seems like we're at an amusement park and there's a mark that says you have to be this tall to go on this ride, or have these certain qualifications to be accepted. But what really is the church, the body of Christ?

The church is made up of every born again believer in the whole world, a group of people with the same vision and goal, committed to spreading the kingdom of God here on earth, until this world is reached for Jesus Christ. The body of Christ is not a pleasure cruiser on its way to Heaven, but a battleship stationed at the very gates of Hell.

6. Love and the Law

I have always thought that it would be cool to be famous for breaking some worldwide record and be in the "Guinese Book of World Records". It wouldn't have to be for anything painful or very stressing, just something that no one else had done. So a few months ago, I challenged myself to get the concordance and go through the whole Bible underlining and studying every single verse that has to do with the law of God. It took me a whole day (from morning to night), an empty gel pin, and a terrible writers cramp, to underline over 515 verses about the law in the Bible! I didn't make it to the "Guinness Book of World Records", but I *did* discover one of the deepest, richest diamond mines in Scripture, not very many have bothered do dig for. Another important skill of a good fisherman in catching fish is to *know what bait to use.*

One of the most important things we have to take in consideration in dealing with sinners, is to aim for *repentance* rather than a *decision*. It's the mentality of modern Christianity to get decisions from sinners. But there's no salvation if there's no true repentance. General Booth said, "The chief danger of the 20th century will be religion without the Holy Spirit, Christianity without Christ, forgiveness without repentance, salvation without regeneration, politics without God, and Heaven without Hell." And that's the point of time we're in. The modern evangelistic message preaches a large, wide door of salvation, but Luke 13:24 says, "*Strive* to enter in at the straight and narrow gait." (My italics).

Did you know that the average "fall-away" rate from local churches to large crusades is about eighty percent?! As I studied the book of Romans and read other books by great revival preachers such as Charles Spurgeon, George Whitefield, Charles Finney, and Jonathan Edwards, I realized that they used a very important principle, which is almost completely forgotten in our modern evangelistic methods.

Psalm 19:7 says, "The law of the Lord is perfect converting the soul." What is perfect in converting the soul? The Law. The law of the Lord is a good thing!

It is the ordinary method of God's Spirit to convict sinners by the Law (which He gave us through the Ten Commandments), because all men "know" that they have sinned, but not all are *convicted* of the guilt of sin.

John Newton, the wretch who wrote "Amazing Grace" said, "My grand point in preaching, is to break the hard heart, and heal the broken one."

You can use the Law to break the hard heart, and Grace to heal the broken one. Let me show you why.

The law shows a sinner what sin is. Romans 7:7 says, "Nay, I had not know sin, but by the law: for I had not known lust, except the law had said, Thou shalt not covet...For without the law sin was dead."

John Bunyan, author of "Pilgrim Progress" said, "The man who does not know the nature of the Law cannot know the nature of sin. And he who doesn't know the nature of sin, cannot know the nature of the Savior."

We have leaned more toward preaching God's grace and love. But one can never feel, know, and appreciate the depth of the ultimate sacrifice paid for by the blood of Jesus Christ on the cross, until one sees his own sinful state and how much he needs that forgiveness and cleansing. As Dwight L. Moody said, "This is what God gives us the Law for, to show us ourselves in our true colors."

1 Corinthians 1:18, "For the preaching of the cross is to them that perish foolishness; but unto us which are saved, it is the power of God."

Do you see how without the law they cannot fully understand or appreciate the Gospel of salvation. But, if you and I follow in the footsteps of Jesus in talking to sinners, when we open up the law (the Ten Commandments) and explain what one has done wrong, they become "convicted by the law as a transgressor", *then* the "Good News" of Jesus Christ will make sense!

Romans 3:19-20 says, "Now we know that what things soever the law saith, it saith...that every mouth may be stopped, and the whole world may become guilty before God. Therefore by the deeds of the law there shall no flesh be justified in his sight: for *by the law is the knowledge of sin*." (My italics)

Nehemiah 8:8-9 tells of an account where he gathered the whole town together and "...they read in the book in the law of God distinctly, and gave the sense, and caused them to understand the reading." Then what happened? "...all the people wept, when they heard the words of the law." The law of God was given to stop proud sinners from justifying themselves because when you go through the Ten Commandments and ask, "Have you ever lied, stolen anything, dishonored your parents...whether they admit it or not, they finally see where they are guilty.

You could say, "Oh, but the preaching of the law is harsh!" *There are gentle ways to say harsh things.* What is even harsher are the consequences of forsaking the law. Proverbs 28:9 says, "He that turneth his ear away from hearing the law, even his prayer shall be an abomination." Then in Jeremiah 6:19 God says, "Hear, O, earth: behold, I will bring evil upon this people, even the fruit of their thoughts, *because they have not hearkened unto...my law, but rejected it*." (my italics)

These are both wake-up calls to us as Christians! Think of what has happened to America since we have closed our ears to the law! It is estimated that there are about 3.5 million teen alcoholics in America, and suicide is the second leading death among youth!

Charles Finney said, "Evermore the Law must prepare the way for the Gospel. To overlook this in instructing souls is almost certain to result in false hope, the introduction of a false Christian experience, and to fill the church with false converts."

This may very well be the reason many people backslide when things didn't go well with them in the Christian life. Because if you have given your heart to Jesus for the right reason (to be safe on Judgment Day, not just to have a happy life) then when problems come, we won't loose your love, joy, peace and backslide, because we didn't come to Jesus for a happier lifestyle but to be safe from Hell fire on Judgment Day!

David knew this well because all throughout the Psalms he says, "The proud have had me greatly in derision: *yet have I not declined from thy law.*" -Psalms 119:51

"The bands of the wicked have robbed me: *but I have not forgotten thy law.*" (v.61)David was having all kinds of problems, yet he never even thought about backsliding and forgetting God's law.

Take a second to think about this. Lets say you had just bought a new car a few days ago. You had just finished washing it, waxing it, and polishing it up, inside and out, and you stood back to take a good look at your work. Then suddenly a big, huge trailer truck comes roaring past you and mud and water goes splattering everywhere all over you and your shinning, clean car. Then you see the windows were rolled down so there was even muddy splashes of water all over your seat covers! Then you notice his mirror also scratched some the paint on your new car.

If a you didn't use foul language and shake your fist at the truck driver guilty of this disaster, and you didn't get all upset about it, lets say someone noticed that and said, "How can you still be so happy? He just messed up your nice, new car!"

Don't try to witness by saying, "Because I have Jesus in my heart and He makes me happy, happy, happy!" Remember what we already said? There are plenty of happy sinners out there!

Say something more along the lines of, "I rejoice because my name is written in Heaven!"

Because if you rejoice because good things are happening to you, then when bad things happen, you'll loose your joy. But if you rejoice because your name is written in Heaven, then *no one* will ever be able to take your joy from you.

You say, "My neighbors and friends wouldn't be interested in God because they already seem to be happy, they've got everything, they just wouldn't be interested." And it's because of this twisted gospel we are preaching that "Jesus makes you happy," we think our feel of evangelical endeavor is just the great misery out there, and not those who are enjoying the pleasures of sin for a season. But I'm telling you there are a lot of happy sinners out there! I was a happy sinner before I came to Christ! That's why You have to circumnavigate the intellect and appeal to their conscience in that they've broken the law (the Ten Commandments) and sinned against a just and Holy God so therefore justice will be done unless they repent.

There is this another thing that appeals to these kind of people and it is the reality of death. As one friend was telling me, "That's what bothered me as a non-Christian. Here I was in this great, big, "happiness bubble", enjoying myself, loving life, but I was also waiting for the sharp pin of reality to break it. I was terrified loosing all this, I couldn't understand how everything on earth I held dear to me, was going to be ripped from my hands by death. I didn't want to die!" For some people, the reality of death is what can be the key that brings them to Eternal life.

Instead of producing a lukewarm decision, such a way of salvation produces a flaming fireball for the Kingdom of God! You and I have the greatest message on earth to deliver! There is always a chance to talk to someone about God. Where you find one that won't listen, you'll find 1,000 that will. Go to the place where you think no one will want to hear what you have to say, find yourself a sinner, and experiment on him!

7. But How?!

"On my account you will be brought before governors and kings as a witnesses to them...do not worry about what to say or how to say it. At that time you will be given what to say, for it will not be you speaking, but the Spirit of your Father speaking through you." —Matthew 10:18-20 (NIV)

Another of the skills of a good fisherman is to *use the right equipment*. Before Communism ruled the country of China, its government leaders were looking for a practical way to penetrate their society with the Communist thinking and way of life. So they searched to develop an effective way to reach their multitudes. Their soldiers watched the men, women and children spending hours reading magazines, comic books, newspaper advertisements, flyers and pamphlets of all different kinds, so they spent millions of dollars printing their propaganda with their philosophies. The results were very successful.

Does this give you any ideas for penetrating *our* world with the gospel?

If you are like 89% of Christians today, you have never

passed out a Christian tract or even directly lead anyone to Christ!

Think of it, most of us are not a real "talking-witness" to those we work with, buy and sell from, to visit with, live next door to, meet at church, or go to school with. But if you don't talk to them, who will? And you know, the hardest thing about talking about God is just bringing the subject up. Most of us can talk about normal things like, "How are you doing", "Nice weather", etc. It's harder to bring God into the picture. And some good news is, tracts do it for you! Far better than you could ever imagine. People actually love them. They will even ask you for more, it has already happened to me many times!

You can even write your own tract. I've done it before. It doesn't have to be a long, complicated, preachy type, just your own life's message about how God saved you, (and no one can contradict you because it is your own life testimony!). Or it could be a story to illustrate salvation, with a catchy phrase.

Putting numbers on things really catches peoples' attention, because they will want to know what those things are. You can become a real effective soul-winner just by handing out tracts (1). You're probably thinking, " Me? A soul winner, using tracts? But how?" Could you slip a Christian tract in the envelope when paying bills? How about in phone booths, on gas pumps, door knobs, on top of mailboxes, on public phones, in public bathrooms (with a rubber band), on school campuses, in taxi cabs, in library books, stick them in elevators, at bus stop benches, in store dressing rooms, at restaurant tables, etc. Have you thought of the fact that so many people are out on the streets passing out their flyers for psychic hot-lines and palm readers, but where are the Christians passing out tracts?

Did you know that if you left 3 tracts in a different place each day, you would reach 1,000 people in only 1 year!

You're probably thinking, "That's is only if they get saved right then and there with the tract." I was thinking that too, but you know what? Whatever you do will be like a seed planted by faith and God's Word will not return void, what an awesome promise He has given us! It is that link in the chain that will bring them to Christ.

You could say, "What if someone says they don't believe in God, they don't believe the Ten Commandments, and they don't believe in the Bible?"

If you come up to me, put a gun to my head and say, "I'm going to pull this trigger", and I laugh and say, "I don't believe in bullets, that thing can't hurt me." I might not live to change my mind! *Unbelief doesn't change reality!* So don't take any notice of people who say, "I'm an atheist, I don't believe the Bible and I don't believe in God." Whether they believe in it or not, it doesn't make any difference. Don't argue about whether or not man came from the ape, instead talk about the reality that we all have a conscience and a knowledge of right and wrong, and will therefore stand without excuse on judgment day. Just go right ahead and be sensitive to the direction of the Spirit.

There are a zillion ways to spread the good news and reach our unsaved friends and relatives, but before everything comes prayer. What do you think of when you heard the word "prayer?" Do you think, "Boring." Or do you think, "This is the incredible privilege that I have of coming into the throne room of God and boldly through faith, asking what I will and gathering the destiny of nations!"

I call it "*prayer-evangelism.*" This is the very *first* step for accomplishing anything in reaching others for Christ. We can see this example in the Bible when God was talking about the children of Israel. "The people of the land have used oppression and exercised robbery, and have vexed the poor and needy...and I sought for a man among them, that should make up the hedge, and stand in the gap before me

The Great Go-Mission

for the land, that I should not destroy it: but I found none."
—Ezekiel 22:29-30

God is looking for people to "stand in the gap!" I'm also thinking about the example in the Deuteronomy 32 where Moses cried out to God saying, "Oh this people have sinned a great sin...yet now if thou wilt forgive their sin—; and if not, blot me, I pray thee, out of thy book..." He stood in the gap for their sins and even went to the extremes of placing his eternal life and salvation in place of their life and salvation! Through prayer you can go to the enemy's camp and take back what he stole, and break the strongholds, so that he will release those souls once taken captive.

I am exited to share with you a true example of this technique of prayer evangelism because I have already tried it and it works!

I have a friend who lives in Europe and he grew up in a good home, but was taught Atheism and Evolution since he was a little boy, so that's what he believed. Since I had met him, I had a big, huge burden on my heart to start praying for him that he would come to know Jesus. So I started praying for him every time I thought of him. It was an urgent prayer, I was just begging God to invade his life twenty-four hours a day and save his life and somehow do this miracle, without me having to play "tug-of-religion" and step in the matter myself. In fact I got so desperate with God, I even started fasting once a week, which I had never before been able to do before!

Time went on, we both lived two countries far apart, but one year he and some friends decided to come visit my country and they stayed at my house. This time I saw him, I saw such a hunger in him for truth, I knew God was working on his heart. I was excited! He would pull any Christian aside to ask him questions about Christianity, God, and the Bible. Now we're talking here about a guy here who calls himself an atheist!

During that time, I had been reading a great book called, "Mere Christianity" by one of my favorite authors, C.S. Lewis. I knew my friend loved books, and that would be a great one for him, but the same time I was debating on whether or not to give him this book now because I wondered if he was ready for it, if he would understand it, or if it would just mix him up more, you know what I mean? I didn't want anything to mess up this "salvation plan!" Then I thought, "Well, I'll just give it to him anyway."

The minute I showed it to him, his eyes lit up and he said, "Oh Cristina, I have been searching for this book all over Europe, but I never found it, and then here you give it to me! Thank you so much!"

I was speechless. And to think that I was that close to not giving it to him, the very key to his salvation! I'm so glad I listened to God about going ahead and giving him that book instead of listening to my "logical" conscience! During that time I had also been reading an incredible book by Ray Comfort entitled, "How to Make an Atheist Backslide", so I couldn't believe what had taken place! It worked! It worked! I was walking on air, I was so thrilled, I just couldn't contain it! After two long years of praying and fasting for him, God had answered my prayer. This was the same guy who had earlier quoted to me Marx's words saying, "Religion is the opium of the people."

Through all this I realized the meaning of the scripture in where it says not to "grow weary in well doing for in due season we shall reap!" When a baby is born, it's not totally a surprise. It begins to grow and develop in the womb for 9 months. It took my friend about three years of "growing and developing in the womb" before he was to be born again and become a Christian. With some people it may take shorter or longer period of time, but don't rush it, or you may produce a "still-born."

We can pray as long and hard as we want, and we should,

(acting at the same time) but without getting weary because when it's God's timing, everything will just perfectly fall into place. I think most of the time, a soul saved and a life changed is the fruit of a praying friend or relative.

8. Be Flexible

"Knowing therefore the terror of the Lord, we persuade men..." -2 Corinthians 5:11

Since we have been exhorted to have speech that is "...always with grace, seasoned with salt..." -Colossians 4:6, it is important that we learn how to accomplish this because we are carriers of the most important message in the world. "Salting" a listener is creating in him a curiosity and interest for what we have to day *before* we say it. Jesus would often create curiosity and interest by asking questions rather than making statements. Be interested in the lives of others, find out what their main beliefs are and what security it gives about going to heaven. I have found out that one of the only differences with Christianity and other false religions in the world, is that Christianity is the only belief that is not based on receiving salvation and eternal life, through works. Let them get hungry, and you can pray for them and provoke them to ask their own questions when they see your "different" Christian lifestyle, which should clearly reflect Jesus. Be such a strong, "salty Christian", and live your life in such a way that the whole world will come thirsting after what you've got! Everyone has heard the saying, "You can lead a horse to water, but you can't make him drink." You can't make him drink, but you can "salt the oats!"

Now I'm not saying, "push Jesus in everyone's face", or most likely they will push it back to you. You don't have to chase after people until you convince them to receive the gospel of Jesus Christ. As a wise man once said, "When fruit is ripe for the picking, it should fall into your hand, and when someone is ready for the Savior, you shouldn't have to jerk them off the tree of the world."

We have to be sensitive to the Holy Spirit with each individual person we witness to, because it's not always going to work if you run up to them saying, "Unless you repent, you will perish!" Instead, sometimes it works just becoming a friend, talking, sharing and showing interest in their life. That's something people everywhere mostly want and need in our world today; someone who will just listen to them, be a true friend, take interest in their lives. Show them you will be there when they need a trustworthy friend. Let them know they have a real friend in you, before you want them to see they have a real friend in Jesus. Be sensitive to God's Spirit and His promptings, and let it shine through you. Just the fact that you take interest in their lives, will speak a multitude of words and cause them to open up their heart to you. But you have to find the balance between loving them and preaching at them. Because different things work for different people.

Charles Spurgeon said, "Don't just throw the seeds at people. Grind it into flour, bake it into bread, and slice it for them. And it wouldn't hurt to put some honey on it."

That's why this issue of "salting" your listeners is very important because you have to be alert and *create the circumstance* to talk to others about Jesus. A wise man once said, "As in farming, a farmer doesn't grow crops. A farmer only creates the conditions for the crops to grow." We could use that in evangelism and say, "As in fishing, a fisherman doesn't *catch* the fish. He only creates the circumstances for the fish to be caught."

As drastic as this may sound, the actual "soul winning" part is not really our responsibility! Our responsibility is to be the example of a Christian, share it with others, spread the good news. Jesus Christ is the one who will go before you, prepare the hearts of your listeners, back you up, and do the unfinished work in their hearts after you have done your part. But don't just sit there waiting for the "perfect" time to come, because you've got about as much a chance of having a sinner visit a church building as you have a criminal visit a police station. It's just not a nice place to go when you're guilty! That's why you have to *go out*! *You* have to create the circumstance!

Milton Berle said, "If opportunity doesn't knock, build a door."

The key to evangelism and presenting the gospel, is that you find the appropriate "wrapping" to effectively deliver the "package".

9. Be Patient and Persevere

Some people are so hard with the gospel that we can get to our "wits end" and think, "Forget it. Why bother?"

A hen will scratch harder when worms are scarce. If souls are scarce, pray more, witness more, get more passion, get more zeal, and you will get your worms, if you "faint not". I remember one time when I was standing in airport lobby waiting to board a plane for Houston, when suddenly in the middle of the waiting room I heard some commotion going on and I turned to see two men who stood up and started to speak in a loud, projecting voice to the whole crowd of people who were also waiting in the lobby. As I listened I realized they were not just any ordinary people, they were Christians and they were telling the story of Jonah! The whole room became silent and people came from everywhere to listen. Meanwhile, the lobby was getting more and more crowded and these men got out some balloons and started molding and shaping them according to their story. And before you knew it, they were giving the whole plan of salvation! The whole room became silent.

The people were awestruck. Toward the end of their testimony, the airline stewardess came up and asked the men if they were still planning to leave on their flight, because the plane was starting to leave! I was astonished and amazed by what I was seeing. In this afternoon in the lobby of that airport, I witnessed something I'll never forget. My heart was so encouraged and challenged by the testimony of those men. They weren't quick to get decisions or lead the people in a prayer, but I can guarantee you that they left a lasting impression on the minds of the people that they will never forget. They weren't dressed up like preachers, they looked like regular "ol' country boys", but they had a big heart for God and a passion for spreading His word and reaching the lost.

Furthermore, always remember that, "God does not call those who are qualified, He qualifies those He calls." - Author unknown

God doesn't require your ability, just your availability. He merely desires a pure, humble, peace-loving, compassionate heart to use as His mouthpiece.

One of the skills of a good fisherman is to *know when to be patient in waiting for results.* Do your part, and leave it up to God to do the rest!

These days, our pursuit—to seek out and save the lost, has to become more desperate and more intense. We have to make it "hard" for people to go to Hell! There is no harder work and none that brings greater results than winning souls.

"Thus saith the Lord...I will go before thee and make the crooked places straight...and I will give thee treasures of darkness, and hidden riches of secret places...I have even called thee by name...though thou hast not known me. I have raise him up in righteousness, and I will direct all his ways: he shall build my city, and he shall let go my captives...men of stature, shall come over unto thee, and they shall be thine: in chains they shall come over, and they shall fall down unto thee, they shall make supplication unto thee, saying, Surely God is in thee; and there is none else, no other God." —Isaiah 45 KJV

What a privilege. What an exciting responsibility to be a Christian alive today! People everywhere are more spiritually open today than any other generation, and we have to find ways to connect and say, "Look, what you are talking about, let me take you to the One who can fulfill it." Many people today are looking for "guides", they are looking for companions, and people to answer their questions about life. We as Christians can get alongside people and as we live vibrant Christian lives, which isn't easy, which takes time, which takes discipline, which is about an everyday relationship with Jesus Christ, then people will be drawn to the one true God, because for many it is the genuine truth they've been searching for. And it will happen gently, it will take time, and it will cost us, but our real heart's desire should be what Paul says, that others may come to the saving knowledge of Jesus Christ. The essence of what God is doing in the world today is gathering men and women from every nation, tribe and tongue, unto Himself to make ready His bride for His second coming. We have to get busy, we don't have time to waste.

You could say, "But I'll *never* be able to go somewhere overseas or anywhere else!" Don't complicate your life! Stop wishing and start fishing! You don't have to leave home to impact the world! God has already placed you in a mission field right where you are, the question is, have you done anything about it? *Then* if you get the privilege of going somewhere else, great!

Reality is, the only thing that will really count at the end of your life, is how many people you have led to the Lord, because the only thing that you and me can take with us into

Eternity is those people who whom we have led to salvation. If God decided your time is over and you were to leave earth today, would you be going empty handed?

One night as I was out looking out at all the stars in the sky (one of my favorite pastimes) I was talking to God and I said, "See all those stars in the sky? That's how many people I want to reach for You. That's how many souls I want to take to heaven with me when I go."

There was a tract written by an atheist which dramatically changed the life of C.T. Studd, helping him turn from lukewarm Christianity to being on fire for God. After reading the tract, he walked away from great financial wealth and being one of the greatest athletes in all of England's history, to become a missionary in China and Africa.

Here is the tract: "Did I firmly believe, as millions say they do, that the knowledge and practice of religion in this life influences destiny in another, religion would mean to me everything? I would cast away all earthly enjoyments as dross, earthly cares as follies, and earthly thoughts and feelings as vanity. I would take thought for the tomorrow of eternity alone. I would esteem one soul gained for Heaven worth a life of suffering. Earthly consequences should never stay my hand, nor seal my lips. I would strive to look upon eternity alone, and on the immortal souls around me, soon to be everlastingly happy or everlastingly miserable. I would go forth to the world and preach it in season and out of season and my text would be: "For what is man profiteth, if he shall gain the whole world, and lose his own soul? Or what shall a man give in exchange for his soul?" —Matthew 16:26

Joseph Alleine, a Puritan preacher from the 16th century, in pleading with sinners he said these words, "But from whence shall I fetch my argument? With what shall I win them? Oh, that I could tell! I would write to them in tears, I would weep out every argument, I would empty my veins for ink, I would petition them on my knees. Oh how thankful would I be if they would be prevailed with to repent and turn."

Listen to the burden on this guy's heart for the lost, he said, "...I would empty my veins for ink!" I wonder how many of us would even empty a ball point pen to warn a relative or an old friend of Judgment Day and their need to come to the Savior.

Charles Spurgeon said, "When I have shot and spent all my gospel bullets and I have none left and little effect seems to be made upon my hearers, I then get in the gun and shoot myself at them." He was saying, when I have preached Jesus to lost sinners and the need they have of a Savior, to escape God's wrath and the very jaws of Hell, when I have preached Christ crucified who bled for them and tell them the good news of the Gospel, and still they stiffen their necks and harden their hearts, then I just open my heart and bleed for them.

"Let him know, that he which converteth the sinner from the error of his way shall save a soul from death, and shall hide a multitude of sins." -James 5:20 Saving a soul from death and eternal torment in Hell is the greatest thing you could do with your life.

Perhaps it will take the Day of Judgment when we see the Master shinning in strength and power, seated on His throne, and before Him from every nation, tribe and tongue, billions of humanity. Then in that vast sea of people, you see someone you witnessed to, someone you gave a tract to, someone you called on the phone, someone you wrote a letter to, and just mentioned that they needed to repent and give their lives to Jesus Christ. Perhaps only then will it really sink into you and me what God was trying to use us for, and that it was worth it all.

8

Four Things We Are *All* Called to Do

Your life calling is not a like a cookie-cutter box, it is just whatever you feel God wants you to do, and you should seek training in that area to see if that really is what God wants you to do. One of the most important and meaningful things you can do in your life is find your life purpose because it will influence everything else you do in your life. Guidance to find your life purpose springs out of your relationship with God, and He promises to guide those who are walking with him. Once you get a good, strong, stable relationship with Jesus Christ, you *will* find your purpose in life, you *will* be fulfilled. Remember, God is more concerned about your future than even you are.

1. Mentor and Develop Disciples

Your probably thinking, "Now the evangelism part

sound easy, but discipleship?!"

A huge part of the Great Commission is to, "Go therefore and make disciples in all the nations...teaching them to observe all things which I have commanded you." — Matthew 28:19

Here we see that one of the last things Jesus told his disciples before He left the earth was to "Go and *make disciples* and *teach* all nations..." You—right now—can *teach* all nations, because if you have already received Jesus in your heart, then you already have something to give the world. You have something that this lost and dying generation needs!

Why do so many people say the sinners' prayer, walk away from the altar (never go on to discipleship) and then backslide? Statistics say that in most evangelistic crusades, there is a 70 to 80 percent "fall-away" rate, and only about 5 percent of all the people actually get into a church where they receive spiritual growth. That's terrible! Because as Christians in evangelism we should do everything we can, not to just get decisions, not to just get church and youth group members, but to produce fruit-bearing commitments to Christ!

Discipleship is something that is very key to evangelism because we can lead others to Christ but, if they don't receive spiritual food, how are they going to strengthen themselves to be able to take the mission on themselves and rescue others from the flames of Hell just as they were rescued?

Not only are we supposed to bring in souls to the Kingdom, but also put them in a place where they can grow and mature and be able to go out and do the same. Then the cycle starts over. You can hydrate a de-hydrated horse but he will just get dehydrated again if you don't lead him to a place where he can find water for himself.

The issue of discipleship is widely talked about, but little carried out. Still I believe discipleship is a very, very important element after winning souls to Jesus, because it is all about building a stronger quality relationship with God and making it contagious.

The word "disciple" means learner, or student, and we are all students under the Master Creator. But what really is this issue of "discipleship?" I think I can explain it very simply: two disciples in a ship. But they aren't just two disciples in a ship. They're spending quality time together, learning from each other, teaching each other, and discipling each other. Like "soul-friends," which is pretty much someone who is like a spiritual advisor, someone whom you could go to and they could keep you accountable and "on track", in terms of what a Kingdom-focused life is really meant to be like. If we fail to demonstrate a quality of life greater than that which the world already experiences, then when will things change?

If our lives fail to reflect the answers Jesus Christ offers to all the world's questions, then what are we really saying to the world, and society?

Being a disciple wasn't just for His twelve, it is for everyone who seeks to grow more and climb to a higher level in their walk with God.

Paul was a master discipler. He carried on intimate fellowship with those whom he led to Christ, and they had intimate fellowship with him. He prayed for his disciples daily and wrote letters to them from which all benefit today. He freely acknowledged that he had not yet reached perfection, yet the commitment he had for his disciples motivated him to die to himself and experience all the suffering he went through, to bring them to spiritual maturity and to produce the character of Christ in them.

That is why we don't need to wait until we're perfect to make disciples, because we are not making disciples unto ourselves, but rather unto Christ. Our credibility is not in what *we* have achieved, but in what *Christ* did for us through his life, death, and resurrection.

Many times we don't think of the fact that Jesus usually worked with a group. Jesus didn't come and change the world on His own, He got together a team. Out of all the crowds of people He talked to and ministered to, He chose twelve disciples in whom He invested a lot of time, energy, and effort into. When Jesus chose His group of disciples, they were, in the eyes of the world, some of the most "weird, ignorant, insignificant, and unlearned" men, and compared to Jesus they were like a wire all messed up and bent out of shape! Yet these men later became some of the most powerful communicators in history. He actually only spent about three years Himself doing ministry, then He left those disciples to go and carry on and actually bear most of the fruit. But it wasn't just time spent working together, they were friends together, developing a true friendship, and more than that, they enjoyed life together. They had times of fun, fellowship, and celebration.

In the Bible days, Jesus attracted many crowds of people, calling them to follow Him. Some followed closer than others, like the twelve disciples, and Jesus seemed to be content for people to follow at their own pace and distance, but the closer the people were to Jesus the more they became like Him. It works the same with us today. The closer we get to Jesus, the more we will become like Him. But it all depends on us.

I once read the saying, "Sometimes more comes by formation than information." Christ shared with others from His heart, not just a dry religion preached with words, and others learned from His perfect example. It's not about head knowledge, it's about practically applying all that we have learned and coming alongside others to lift them up and serve them. It is about going out and making mature disciples who will be more effective for His kingdom.

There are many things that we do, that make sense, but

Four Things We Are All *Called to Do*

don't work. The things God does, don't make sense, but work! Jesus did things differently. I feel that God is now bringing a "new approach" to this generation, and we have to learn from the past and be open to the Holy Spirit to lead us and guide us. There's a strategy straight from God's heart, lead by His Spirit, that we have to get a hold of. We need new approaches to the mission that God has called us. It's not about numbers, it's about faithfulness. Discipleship is not about quantity, but about quality. It's not about counting nickels and noses, lets get to the core of what's really important! We have been so obsessed with numbers, the average question when you go to another church is, "So how big is your group?" A father will be judged on his success as a son, Dad, husband, Christian, etc., not on how many children he gave birth to. Anyone can have children, but his success will be on how he did with those God gave him. If someone would have asked Jesus, "So Jesus, how big is your group?" He probably would have said, "Well, I've got three guys who I'm really close to, then there are nine whom I've given most of myself to, there are about another seventy-two who I spend a lot of time with. But to be honest with you, my flock is the whole of Israel, the whole of the world."

In the same way we have a few people who are our best friends, maybe a bigger group whom we spend time with at school and church, but we also have a few thousand more people in our city which we are responsible for, who don't yet know Jesus. They aren't numbers, they are precious, eternal souls! Our values have to change, it's not about how big a group we have, it's not about size and number, it's about recognizing that we are called to shepherd sheep who are harassed, helpless, and torn apart. The early days in a Christian's walk with God are the days of greatest vulnerability, and the enemy wants to snatch away the precious seed that has been planted, as it says in Matthew 13. We have to be there for them and quickly pick them up when they go down. At any age we're at, in any stage in our walk with the Lord, we all still need to disciple and be discipled. A church cannot grow and achieve its goals without it. Just as you have to find the balance of giving and receiving, you can be discipled and at the same time disciple others.

There is one extremely important element in accomplishing this calling of effective evangelism and discipleship: unity. Together we stand; divided we fall. It is as plain and simple as that. There is not any more time to be playing around fussing and fighting as goes on in many churches today. We have to renew our false mentality of, "this is my church" etc. and instead it be "this is a part of the whole body of Christ." We must work together rather than competing. Discipleship is not about, "I'm the leader and all of you just follow and submit." It's about helping others in their relationship with Jesus, because a true disciple points others to Jesus for all the answers. We need each other, we cannot be independent Christians. The Christian life is all about running the race *together*. I too am running the race with you! We have only just begun. We cannot be a "closed system."

Closed systems die. We are composed of many parts, but all one body. As Christians, we are supposed to bring encouragement to our other fellow brothers and sisters in Christ, that's part of what discipleship is all about.

Each one of us is called to take our responsibility seriously. Many new things will be birthed as you allow God to work in your heart and allow Him to plant some seeds in there that will spring to life. The place were Christian youth are really growing spiritually is a place were true discipleship is taking place. When you find an environment of faith and encouragement, those things will begin to bear fruit. That's what we're looking for, that we will see thousands of people come to know Jesus and grow in him and it's all because Jesus is worth it, it's all because people all around desperately need you and me to take our responsibility seriously and make the difference. It's up to us to make it happen. Everything starts with being faithful in the small things. Revolutions don't take place over-night, but after persevering and fighting the battle long and hard. Battles can be good, because if you're still struggling, then you haven't been beat!

Luke 4:18-19 says, "The spirit of the Lord is upon me, because he has anointed me to preach the good news to the poor. He has sent me to proclaim freedom for the prisoners and recovery of sight for the blind, to release the oppressed, to proclaim the year of the Lord's favor."

Re-read this scripture to yourself out loud, declare it over your life, personalize it, believe in it, and make it a true reality for your life. The world needs a billion and more people like this, who truly walk in Jesus' shoes. Someday when you and I appear before the Lord, He isn't going to be interested in the academic degrees we achieved or the jobs we worked at, He will want to know how many people we have brought into the kingdom, and how many we discipled. As drastic as this may sound, Jesus doesn't want decisions, He wants disciples.

2. We are all called unto Holiness

Two older women from Southern California were about to cross the Mexican border to return to America, when they saw what looked like a very small sick animal in the ditch beside their car. As they examined it in the darkness of the night, they saw that it was a tiny Chihuahua. Then and there they decided to take it back to America and nurse it back to health. However because they were afraid to get caught breaking the law, they wrapped it in a blanket, put it in the trunk of the car, and drove across the border. Once they were in America, they retrieved the animal and nursed it until they arrived home.

One of the women was so concerned for the ailing dog she actually let it sleep in the bed with her, and reached out at different times during the night to touch the tiny animal and reassure it that she was still present. The dog was so sick the next morning, she decided to take it to the veterinarian. That's when she found out that the animal wasn't a tiny, sick Chihuahua. It was a Mexican water rat, dying of rabies!

The world in the blindness and blackness of its ignorance treats sin like it's a puppy to be played with. It is the light of God's Law that enlightens the sinner to the fact that he is actually in bed with a deadly rat. We have to be even *more* grossed out with the rat of sin as you were grossed out by the rat in this story.

Its Friday night and all your best buds are coming over to watch the Super Bowl. You know how it goes when they all get together, everyone has their favorite player whom they want to be like in the game (you can probably tell I've got brothers!). We have all spent hours watching our favorite players. You've studied their moves, the way they celebrate a great play—you even know what type of deodorant and brand of socks they are currently sporting!

But these people didn't become great athletes just because they learned how to respond in a certain way during the game. Sorry, but the deodorant and Gatorade is not the key to greatness! These "heroes" are great because of a lifestyle of discipline. They have dedicated their lives to train and prepare. They sacrifice sleep to get up early and train. And when everyone else has gone home, they are still practicing or working on areas to improve. When their friends are just chilling at the mall, they are shooting baskets over and over, or running miles to get in top condition. It is a whole lifestyle of preparation of mind and body to provide a foundation for their responses in the game. We can't hope to be like "the great ones" just by copying their moves during a game, because that's not how they became great.

Four Things We Are All Called to Do

Jesus has called us all to live holy lives. No, that doesn't mean He wants us to become monks and nuns and go find the closest monastery to move in. The holiness He requires of us is something practical in our daily living, not mystical. Holiness is not separation from *sinners*, but from *sin*. Like Jesus we should be a "friend" of sinners, yet remain untainted by the things of this world. As Christians we are to be set apart from the actions of the world and live lives of purity dedicated to Him-just as a great athlete rises above and is set apart from the others. Leonard Ravenhill said, "Let no man think of fighting Hell's legions if he is still fighting an internal warfare. Carnage without will sicken him if he has carnality within. It is the man who has surrendered to the Lord who will never surrender to his enemies."

We won't be able to respond to life's everyday situations in a right way if we are not properly prepared. Just as the great sports hero would not be able to make the great shot when the pressure of the moment was upon him if he didn't have the lifestyle of preparation. If you live your life trying to be as much like the world as possible yet remain a Christian, when you find yourself in tense situations, you will fail. Because it just doesn't work that way. God wants you to be *blindly* holy in your home, school, church, and youth group, not falling back into sameness but making your mark as a difference in this life.

"…that we…might serve him in holiness and righteousness before him, all the days of our lives." —Luke 1:74-75 KJV

In the concordance, this Greek word for holiness, is *"hosios"*, which refers to "having divine character and being distinguished in human statutes and relations." Just like with the athlete, it's all about our character, and the difference we make in our actions and relationships with others.

I am very aware that now in this generation God has

been raising up many great, young musicians and worshippers of God to lead His people, and this is a very beautiful and honorable position in ministry, but there is one, very important element (that many of us have forgotten) which He requires of us...holiness.

I found about five times in the Bible (1 Chronicles. 16:29, 2 Chronicles. 20:21, 31:18, Psalm 29:2, 96:9) where our worship is directly linked with the holiness in our lives.

Psalm 96:6 says, "O worship the Lord in the beauty of holiness..." Worship is much more meaningful and beautiful when it is done in holiness because true worship flows from a heart that cries out for holiness. As it says in Joshua 3:5, "Consecrate yourselves, for tomorrow the Lord will do amazing things among you."

3. We are all called to be Worshipers of God

If someone were to come up now and ask you the question, "What is worship?" How would you explain it to them? Take a pause in this book and think for just one second. What does "worship" mean to you? What does it bring to mind?

Calvin Coolidge once said, "Reverence (worship) is the measure, not of others, but of ourselves...what men worship is what they become (like)." Isaiah 6:1-8, gives a wonderful account of a man who truly experienced the presence of God in an extraordinary way, because of having the heart of a worshipper. This man was Isaiah and here is his story.

"In the year king Uzziah died, I saw the Lord seated on a throne, high and exalted, and the trains of his robe filled the temple. Above him where seraphs, each with six wings: With two wings they covered their faces, with two they covered their feet, and with two they were flying. And they were calling to one another: "Holy, holy, holy is the Lord

Four Things We Are All Called to Do

Almighty; the whole earth is full of his glory."

The first thing that happened was Isaiah saw God in all His glory and all the angels round about Him singing to each other 'Holy is the Lord and the whole earth is full of His glory'. Then he understood how powerful and glorious and mighty God is. Many times we tend to bring God down to our level as our buddy and friend, but we should never forget that He is so much more than that, He is our Holy Lord and awesome Creator!

"At the sound of their voices the doorposts and thresholds shook and the temple was filled with smoke. "Woe to me!" I cried. "I am ruined! For I am a man of unclean lips, and I live among a people of unclean lips, and my eyes have seen the King, the Lord Almighty."

But it didn't stop there, Isaiah didn't just see, hear and feel God, it brought him to act. He was overwhelmed by the presence of God and humbled himself and recognized that he was a man of "unclean lips" and that he was not worthy to be standing in the presence of an almighty God, and then he proclaimed the Lord's name and exalted Him.

"Then one of the seraphs flew to me with a live coal in his hand, which he had taken with tongs from the altar. With it he touched my mouth and said, "See, this has touched your lips; your guilt is taken away and your sin is atoned for." The Lord sent an angel to him to cleanse him of his unrighteousness and his guilt was taken away and his sin was atoned for.

"Then I heard the voice of the Lord saying, "Whom shall I send? And who will go for us?" And I said, "Here am I. Send me!" One thing that really stands out in my mind, of this scripture, is that Isaiah didn't stay there worshipping God forever, which would have been a wonderful thing.

I've seen so many wonderful Christian people that are so happy-go-lucky and fun to be around, but when they get to church, they just sit there and do nothing. Many people just come in to the church services for the music and just sit there waiting for God to just "show up" and do all the work. However it works the other way around. He is waiting for us to cry out to Him like Isaiah did! Isaiah was excited to be in the house of his God! He couldn't wait to get there and he would stay there forever if he could. But God had different plans. After cleansing Isaiah, the Lord asked him: "Whom shall I send? And who will go for me?"

He was asking to see if Isaiah had a willing heart to go out and do anything God told him. All that Isaiah experienced in the presence of God, brought him to act, and right away he said, "Here I am. Send me!" Here's where evangelism comes in the picture. His quick response to God is important for us to notice because I don't see a picture of him saying, "God, here I am, take me where you want…but just don't send me anywhere far. Don't make me have to go without my friends. Please don't make me have to do anything I won't want to do." How many times are we like that? Isaiah didn't give God any complaints or conditions. I see a picture of him shouting it out to God, "Here I am! Send me!"

Our worship to God must go deeper than the just surface emotions, it has to be a life changing experience, just like what happened to Isaiah; a life changing experience that will give us new direction and guidance to then go out and share with others our experience.

When you connect others to a sense of who God really is, lives are touched and transformed, and many give their lives to Christ.

David's worship is also another key illustration that can be applied in our lives. David's worship was uncompromising and it witnessed of the Lord. David's worship was the kind of worship that had to do with his everyday life, and his personal walk with the Lord not just a Sunday morning thing. Not just on Sunday morning was he busy writing psalms to the Lord. And you don't need anything else except God, you, and your heart, to worship God. Do you think that David was special in God's heart because of his great musical ability? Definitely not, it was because of his obedience and worship before God.

There is not one single person on the face of this earth who has and could truly experienced the God's holy, powerful presence and say, "I don't want it." When you experience the true, Holy presence of Almighty God, you will find something you can't find anywhere else in the world.

I'm also thinking of the example of Paul and Silas when they were in prison. They were true worshippers because they worshipped no matter what their circumstances were. They praised and glorified God as they were being beaten, insulted, mocked at, humiliated, starved, and tortured. I'm wondering how many of us could do that?

Reality is that most of our worship to God is only on Sunday morning and when we go to church. God wants so much more than that. He wants it to be spontaneous where we do it wherever we are, whenever, because it is supposed to come from the abundance of our hearts. Your worship should be an overflow of who you are, something that you are ready to do anytime, anywhere, with anyone.

4. We are all called to Forgive

When I say "called", I really mean "commanded!" The word "forgiveness" sounds nice and most of the time brings a pretty picture in mind, until we think of someone whom we have not yet forgiven. Am I right? Most of you are probably thinking, "Oh, but you don't know how he/she has offended and hurt me!"

Un-forgiveness is one of the most destructive forces in the universe. And when we allow un-forgiveness to creep into our lives we are setting in motion a chain of circumstances that result in spiritual, emotional, relational and physical, destruction.

How many churches, businesses, families and marriages have collapsed because of unresolved conflicts? How many new ailments and deadly disease have come up now days, that were unheard of before, and surprisingly the root cause is un-forgiveness? Just like with King David's example, how many preachers, teachers, and great men and women have fallen into deeper sin and lost their ministries and their families because they didn't humble themselves and ask forgiveness.

In the Lord's prayer we say, "...forgive us our trespasses *as we forgive those who trespass against us.*" But how many of us actually stop and think of what we are saying? According to my paraphrased version it means, "Forgive us all the times we have offended You and others, in the same measure and extent that we forgive all those who have offended us." Forgiveness is so important because it is for the sake of the offended as much as it is the offender. In the degree that we are willing to forgive others, God will forgive us. A wise man once said, "Forgive me and you heal yourself. Tolerate me, and you invite more offense." Forgiveness is the act of believing the Word of God and making the conscience choice to release your offender from your desire of revenge.

The truth is as Proverbs 19:11 says, "The discretion of a man deferreth his anger; and it is his glory to pass over a transgression."

On a favorite cartoon called the Veggie Tales, there is an episode about forgiveness where an "advertiser" comes out advertising a machine called the "Forgive-o-matic". You are just supposed to confess your "sins" into the machine, turn some knobs, push some buttons and presto! You are forgiven! If only it were that easy! Unfortunately it's not, because it doesn't have to do with a machine, but the person we offended.

At one point in my life I began teaching fifth and sixth graders in an English class. The students knew all the rules and what was expected of them during class time, and as the typically "in-class correction" that teachers have done for centuries, I would write down their name on the chalkboard and then put a mark by it every time they would purposely be disobedient or disruptive. After about five marks, I would happily escort them to the principle's office. This helped a lot in discipline because it's not a very pleasant thing for you to see your name written on the chalkboard with some marks beside it! I'm telling you all this because God does the same thing with us. Every time you sin or mess up in something, God puts a mark by your name on His chalkboard. But…when you humble yourself and ask forgiveness of Him first of all, and then whoever else was involved, He completely erases that blackboard with all your sins and He totally forgets them! There is one thing, I found, God can't do. He can't remember past forgiven faults. If you messed up again and came back to God with a repentant heart saying, "God, I'm so sorry I've messed up again." He would probably say, "What do you mean, "messed up again?" For me this is the first time you've done it." He forgets them and separates them as far as the east is from the west!

C.S. Lewis, the famous, intellectual, English writer deals with this subject quite well in his book, "Mere Christianity". He reminds us that one of the greatest commandments is to "…love thy neighbor as thyself." Then he goes on to say, "Because in Christian morals "thy neighbor" includes "thy enemy". So we come up against this terrible duty of forgiving our enemies. Well, how exactly do I love myself? Now that I come to think of it, I do not exactly have a feeling of fondness or affection for myself, and I do not even always enjoy my own society. So apparently "Love your neighbor" does not mean "feel fond of him" or "find him attractive". This is an enormous relief. A good many people imagine that forgiving your enemies means making out that they are really not such bad fellows after all, when it is quite plain that they are. This is what is meant in the Bible by loving him: wishing his good, not feeling fond of him nor saying he is nice when he is not. I admit that this means loving people who have nothing lovable about them. But then, has oneself anything lovable about it? You love it simply because it is yourself. God intends us to love all selves in the same way and for the same reason: but He has given us the sum ready worked out on our own case to show us how it works. We have then to go on and apply the rule to all other selves. Perhaps it makes it easier if we remember that is how He loves us. Not for any nice, attractive qualities we think we have but just because we are the things called selves."

Remember the story of Jacob and Esau when they reconciled? Jacob sent hundreds of sheep, cattle, servants ahead of him as a gift for his brother before he himself came. I think that true forgiveness comes when you can do something *good* for your enemy. Because true forgiveness come when you can take it as a challenge to go the extra mile and invest your time and effort in that person. We have to forgive not because we feel like it, not because the other person deserves it, but because God's forgiveness was sufficient for us at the cross, and we have the command to go and do the same.

Jesus Christ was the perfect example for us in forgiveness unto death, when some of His last words were, "Father, forgive them; for they know not what they do." -Luke 23:34 KJV

9

Nine Ways to Find Your Specific Life Calling

"Therefore, my brothers, be all the more eager to make your calling and election sure. For if you do these things you will never fall..." -2 Peter 1:10

1. Taste Jesus

At a university of a Chicago school each year they have a special event where they would invite one of the greatest minds to lecture in the theological education center. One year they invited Dr. Alexander Tillisch. Dr. Tillisch spoke for two in a half hours on a subject quite discussed that time, proving that Jesus and the resurrection was false. He quoted scholar after scholar, and book after book. He concluded that since there was no such thing as the "historical" resurrection, then the "religious tradition" of the church was just groundless, emotional mumbo-jumbo, because it was based on a relationship with a risen Jesus, who, in fact, "never rose from the dead" in any literal sense. He then asked if there were any questions. After about thirty seconds, an old, dark skinned preacher with a head of short-cropped, wholly white hair stood up in the back of the auditorium. "Docta Tillisch, I got one question," he said as all eyes turned toward him. He reached into his sack lunch, pulled out an apple and began eating it. "Docta Tillisch...crunch, munch...my question is a simple question...crunch, crunch...Now I ain't nevuh read them books you read...crunch, munch...I don't know nothin' 'bout Niebuhr or Heidegger." ...crunch, munch... He finished the apple. "All I want to know is: this apple I jus ate, was it bitter or sweet?" Dr. Tillisch paused for a moment and answered in exemplary scholarly fashion: "I cannot possibly answer that question, for I haven't tasted your apple."

The white haired preacher dropped the core of his apple back into the crumpled paper bag, looked at Dr. Tillisch and calmly said, "Neither have you tasted my Jesus."

The one thousand plus in attendance could not contain themselves. The auditorium erupted with applause and cheers. Dr. Tillisch thanked his audience and promptly left the platform.

Now I want to ask you, "Have you really "tasted" Jesus?" Do you really *know* God? As a person? As a Father? As a friend? It is different to know *about* Him than to really *know* Him. I could tell you all about my friends and their hobbies, their likes and dislikes, etc., but there you still just know *about* them, you don't really know them. And you won't really know them until you meet them, face to face, and share experiences together. We learn from each other by spending time with each other, in the same way we learn from God by spending time with Him.

2. Pray

"Very early in the morning, while it was still dark, Jesus

got up, left the house and went off to a solitary place, where he prayed." -Mark 1:35 NIV

A key thing I see in Jesus' life, was that before making any important, major decisions, He spent at least a whole night in prayer. Before He even initiated His ministry, He spent forty days of prayer and fasting out in the wilderness. I look back on my life and the lives of my friends and I think, "How many fewer wrong decisions would we make if we had spent forty days out in the wilderness, before making that decision?" If we see a need or have the ability to do something we often think we've got to get out there and do it. We have a tendency to just dive in with both feet before we've really thought much about it. It gets even harder for us in a world like today where everything says to "just do it" and go faster and faster and *not* take the time off. Really, the busier we get, the less open and sensitive we are to hearing God's voice. It's really only when we take time to be quiet, rest and reflect, and just allow God to speak to us, that we really do hear His voice.

Do you want to know God's will for your life? Pray. Your prayer life is one of the most important things in your relationship with God, because prayer is the line of communication you have with Headquarters. You can get on the phone and call a friend, but when you can get on your knees and call on God, something supernatural happens in the heavens! Because when you pray, you are actually talking to the most important Being in the whole universe, communicating at your level, with someone on the highest level on earth! (And you don't even need Internet to do it!)

But strangely enough, prayer is not really that easy. I envy people who can get up early and pray for hours on end, or go to prayer vigils and pray all night without falling asleep! Because for me it's like with a person who decides he wants to get his physical body in shape, and he decides he is going to get up every morning and run a few miles or go to the gym and start lifting weights. The first few times you start to do it, it's going to be very difficult and strenuous, but if you give up right then, you will never reach your goal. I was once reading a biography about Martin Luther and how he got up at 4 AM every morning to pray. I'm all excited and charged up about this new so and I say, "I'm going to get up every morning at 6 AM to pray." That's a great idea! But when that alarm goes off, and after it gets pounded for doing its job, if I lay there one minute longer or think I'm too tired and it can be done another day, then again, this goal will never be reached. Most of us will probably admit we don't do enough exercise to stay healthy, and it's the same way with prayer, we don't do enough prayer, to stay spiritually healthy.

Daniel had major responsibilities as the lead president of a world empire. Yet, three times a day he set aside time to go into his "prayer closet" and just pray and worship God. The resulting success in Daniel's life and ministry shows the importance of following his example. There even came a time in Daniel's life when he was prohibited to pray, just like happens today in many public places. When Daniel faced the choice between obeying God and praying, or confronting adversity, he chose to obey God and trust Him for the final outcome. Daniel made a wise decision and he paid the consequences, but God was always with him through every step of the way. As a result of Daniel's testimony of true righteousness even if it could cost him his life, the king came to trust God also.

"Elijah was a man just like us. He prayed earnestly that it would not rain, and it did not rain on the land for three and a half years. Again he prayed, and the heavens gave rain, and the earth produced its crops." —James 5:17-18

Elijah was such a powerful prayer warrior that so moved the heart of God, that God even held back the rain for three years! Because of Elijah's earnest prayers. Think of all the spiritual changes that could occur in this world if all of us would become more powerful prayer warriors just like Elijah.

Picture this...what would you think if you saw a father who gave his son everything he wanted and even sent him to a school on the other side of the world so that he could receive a "higher education" ...but never contacted him just to talk? Sometimes that's how we are. We ask and ask God, but when do we take time out to just talk with Him? How often do you just tell God all about your day?

Learning to pour your heart out to God is something that develops, as your relationship with Him deepens. If we could just take more time to talk to God, get in touch with His heart and daily walk in a spirit of prayer, I know that our "problems" would be like nothing. As I already said, you and I are ambassadors with a mission to carry out here on earth. Just as an ambassador maintains constant communication with the government he is representing, we are to maintain that same daily, intense, and constant communication with the president of the Heavenly government we are representing.

Prayer is at the heart of Christianity, because at the heart of Christianity is a relationship with God. If you're going to get the victory in any area of your life, it's going to have to start with prayer. You will be so much more victorious living in a life of prayer, just because the battle is not by flesh and blood, but by the spirit. Satan laughs at our words, mocks our toil, but trembles when we pray.

3. Develop A Mission Statement

"Thus saith the Lord...I will go before thee and make the crooked places straight...and I will give thee treasures of darkness, and hidden riches of secret places...I have even called thee by name…though thou hast not known me. I have raise him up in righteousness, and I will direct all his ways: he shall build my city, and he shall let go my captives…men of stature, shall come over unto thee, and they shall be thine: in chains they shall come over, and they shall fall down unto thee, they shall make supplication unto thee, saying, Surely God is in thee; and there is none else, no other God." —Isaiah 45 KJV

Many of us have very little understanding of what the Kingdom of God is all about and what part each of us play in it. In our daily walk with God, we have to intentionally decide that we're going to follow Jesus, and not just that but also seek to follow the purposes and plans of God's Kingdom for our lives. One practical thing we can do to get a better focus of this, is developing what I call a "mission statement" for your life. To develop a mission statement I would suggest you do some Biblical study, go through the gospels and look at what the Kingdom of God is all about, ask yourself what His purposes for mankind are, what are His purposes for you, what is God all about in this world today. Then we are to ask ourselves, in what ways has God specifically gifted us to be able to be a part of His Kingdom. Out of that is where you develop a mission statement. It can also help even more if every morning you read your mission statement and ask yourself, "How today, do I want my life to reflect God's mission statement for my life?" It's also very helpful that at the end of every week you pause and reflect on the week that has past and look ahead to the week that is coming and see how well your life is truly reflecting that mission statement in accordance with God's will for you. Just as an example, one of my "mission statements" is the first scripture in this chapter, among many others such as that of the great commission.

It's so easy to let things around us distract us, there are so many messages today coming at us from the secular culture in the world around us and we are constantly being bombarded by them. It's like the world is trying to "brand" us in a way that says we belong to it. I am convinced that unless we are "branded" with strong convictions of God's purposes for our lives, then we can very easily get caught up in the purposes of the world's mentality and culture which surrounds us. In fact, over the last few years, even corporations and businesses have literally gone from selling products, to really trying to sell identity, purpose, and image. Without realizing it, we all buy into these kind of values. If we don't have a stronger message coming from a deep Biblical foundation then I can tell you, we will very quickly be "eaten alive" by the secular culture and world around us. We must be careful not to "drink in " the philosophies of the world through TV., Internet, school, radio, books, movies, friends, and any other thing tainted with humanism or other pernicious doctrines. Just as an airplane can carry good and bad things, these mediums can be transmitters of the good as well as the bad, we have to be very careful.

"Ye shall know them by their fruits. Do men gather grapes of thorns, or figs of thistles? Even so every good tree bringeth forth good fruit; but a corrupt tree bringeth forth evil fruit... Wherefore by their fruits ye shall know them."
—Matthew 7:15-20

4. Listen and Share with your Parents

Do you want to find your purpose in life? Do you want God's best for your life? God gives us an important (but often overlooked) key to accomplishing this in Deuteronomy 5: 16 which says, "Honor your father and mother, as the Lord your God has commanded you, so that you may live long and that it may go well with you..."

The following is a true testimony from a young guy about the important of obedience.

"One day as I was walking out the door to go to high school, my mom called out to me, 'Come straight home after school today'. Then she called out my name again as if she had something else to say, so I stopped. She walked over to me, put her hand on my shoulder, looked me in the eyes, and said, 'I have something very important to do today, so I want you to come straight home after school. Do you understand?' She had never done this before. I said, 'Yes', and walked out the door. I didn't think about it anymore.

After school I went out of the building with two of my friends, one of them turned to me and said, 'I've been over to your house lots of times, but you never come to mine, so why don't you come home with me?' Without thinking, I said 'Okay!' and hopped on the back of his motorcycle. Before the wheels had turned once, the event of that morning and my mother's words came back to me, so I said, "Wait! Wait! I can't go. My mom told me to come straight home after school today.' My other friend said, 'I'll go, I'll go!' So I hopped off and he hopped on, and off they went. I remember standing there and watching them ride off. I was mad at my mom. What made matters worse was that when I got home, my mom wasn't there. I waited and waited. The longer I waited the madder I got.

Finally, she pulled into the driveway at five o'clock. I was really hot by then. I said, 'Where have you been?! You told me to come straight home, and you weren't even here! She said, 'On the way home there was a terrible accident. I didn't see it happen, but the man in the car right in front of me did. One of your classmates was killed, and the other might die. A drunk driver had swerved in front of their motorcycle and hit them head on. The motorcycle driver was catapulted over the car, breaking both his legs where they hit the handle bars. The rider (the guy who took my place on the motorcycle) went flying up in the air as high as a telephone pole, and came down landing on the handle bars which went right through his body. He died an agonizing death there. It took three men to hold him down.' I knew that would have been me. The exchange at school had taken less than five seconds, but if I had not obeyed my mom's words, I would not be alive today and my mom would have witnessed my own death."

Proverbs 30:17 says, "The eye that mocks a father, that scorns obedience to a mother, will be plucked out by the ravens of the valley, will be eaten by the vultures."

The birth of Samson was announced by an angel, and God himself explained the purpose for his life. His parents took special precautions for him to be sure to fulfill this calling of God on his life. However even after all this, God's judgment came on Samson because of his disobedience. It all started out when he was younger and he dishonored his parents and dishonored God, breaking the commands He had given him from birth. First he was bound, both by his lusts and by the trap Delilah set for him. But I ask myself, "How could he have been deceived by her over and over again? How could he fall in the *same* hole again and again? Couldn't he see the trap after a few falls and change his direction?"

The answer is in Proverbs 20: 20 which says, "If a man curses his father or mother, his lamp will be put out in pitch darkness."

Many times we think, "Well I would never curse my parents!" The word here for "curse," actually mean "lightly esteem." Remember the story of Samson in the Bible? Many times I have wondered how Samson could be deceived over and over by the same woman?!

I mean, wouldn't he have realized that she was helping the Philistines capture him, after so many times of trying? Samson was in "pitch darkness" as a consequence of his disobedience and lightly esteeming his parents. When someone is in the dark, he can't see where he is going and he will fall in the same hole over and over without realizing it. It doesn't take a rocket scientist to find that out! First Samson was "blinded" by his dishonor and disobedience, next Samson was blinded by his enemies. Before they put out his physical eyes, his spiritual eyes had already been "plucked out," he was already suffering from spiritual blindness. He was then forced to grind in prison with shame, with God's enemies mocking him. The very same people God had given him power to rule over, were now trampling him under their feet.

Listening and sharing with your parents is so important because they can give you so much help and direction in times of need. They have watched you grow up, they know your strengths and weaknesses, and they can help you see your life from the bigger picture. Your parents have already lived out their teen years and they can look back and see the mistakes they made and help you not to fall in the same hole. You can learn from your parents and take notes on your "mental note pad" of life.

As a little side note to you parents. The best advice I could ever give you in raising a family is this: learn to enjoy your children! Invest your *life* into your children, not just your money. Don't let them become passing strangers in the home. I can say that most of everything that I've learned and written in this book was through morning devotions, mealtime conversations and living experiences with my family. The strength of a nation is in its families.

Each and every family is the "perfect" family because God created it just like He wanted it to be, with each family member with the character that they need to mold and shape each other's lives. Believe it or not, God has put you in the perfect family with the right brothers and sisters, where He is teaching, training, and preparing you for your future calling in life.

God uses our siblings and parents to mold our character to be as more like what God wants it to be. When we don't allow Him to mold us in this way, He will be sure to do it another way, through other authorities, teachers, classmates, and even one's future life's mate. Of one thing you can be sure, God never makes mistakes! He is the Master of perfection.

Think of Joseph. Throughout all the hardships he went through as a young boy, God was using them all along to prepare him for his future work. Did Joseph know that? No. But if he would have started to complain and ask God "Why me?!" Do you think the story would have had the same ending? No.

Think about Peter. God put him in a home where his Dad was a fisherman, because later in life Peter was to become a fisher of men. He put David in a home where he was a shepherd and cared over a flock of sheep which was training for him to later be a "shepherd" over the whole "flock" of Israel. This aspect is so important in life because I have seen many great Christian people that love God and really have a passion for Him, but yet in their family and home life, they fight with their parents and can never get along with their siblings. You can't imagine how much this hinders and dilutes their effectiveness in their goals, vision, and ministry to others.

I remember when my brothers were younger, they loved to wrestle and "beat each other up". Now we laugh and say, "That was training for when you become a missionary and get beat up by the natives!" You can be sure of one thing, if you can learn to get along with the people in your family, then you will be able to get along with anyone in the whole world!

If you're in circumstances where you don't have your parents close by, I urge you to look for some older, mature authority (relatives, pastor, counselor, etc.) just someone whom you can talk to and share with and can keep you accountable through your life.

This is a very important factor in life, and even though many times they just don't seem to make sense, whether your parents are saved or not, as you honor them, you are honoring God, and He will honor you for that!

5. Read Biographies

Mark Twain said, "The man who does not read good books has no advantage over the man who can't read." Someone also said, "There are two things that most largely influence your life, the friends you have, and the books you read." So I would encourage you to read good biographies. I think that it can help increase your faith when you can see the lives of other men and women of God and how He used them as they fulfilled their life purpose. You can also spot their mistakes and learn from them. So even if you absolutely hate reading, please give it a try, God will be able to teach you so many new things through reading Christian biographies.

Russel H. Conwell, American author of the inspirational classics, "Acres of Diamonds," has explained the importance of biography in the following words: "History is but the aggregate of individual biographies, and it sometimes happens in the history of great nations that the biography of a single man, comprehensively written, contains all the important history of the government through a series of years. the study of biography in the records of nearly every nation furnishes the surest and easiest means of obtaining certain and lasting information concerning the institutions, character, events, and time. It is, however, in the moral effect upon the readers that the writing and study of biography places its highest claims. It encourages the young, gives hope to the hopeless, warns the careless, cautions the foolish, and by its descent into the little details of practical life furnishes a guide, companion, and counselor to every student.

6. Find out the Meaning of Your Name

The most significant word in any language is one's own name, it's the most important sound to us no matter what the language. Your name is very important to God, yet many people don't have the slightest idea what their name means. The first job God gave Adam in the Garden of Eden was to give a name to all the animals, and each one of their names is related to God's design and purpose for each animal. In the same way, I think it's important that we relate our name with the God-given meanings and characteristics.

Most people tend to live up to their understanding of the name given to them. It is so funny because many times I'll look up a friend's name and see that the definition of it is "right on" with his or her character, looks, or way of acting because there is just something about us that really identifies each one of us with our name. I'm really stressing this point because finding out the positive meaning of your name could greatly help you find greater meaning and purpose as well as give you spiritual guidance in your life.

For example, my younger sister's name is Natalia. It comes from a Latin root meaning "Birth". When my parents first found out the definition of that name, they didn't think it was that great of a meaning, yet they still felt that was the name she should have. After deepening our search for a meaning, we found it meaning "the act of bringing forth off-spring; the original or beginning of something." For us that was a good meaning, but little did we know it would have an even greater meaning when at last minute, Natalia ended up being the only one of our family who was born in our home.

So that was a real significant birth!

I'll give you another example with the well-known name of "Mary". Its root comes from the same root as *myrrh* which means *bitter*. When the myrrh bush is cut it produces "tears". These are then collected and made into essential ingredients for the most fragrant perfumes. These "tears" also have great healing qualities. Can you guess a better definition for that name? We could get many out of these two things but the one I'm thinking of now is, "A sweet and healing fragrance that comes when rightly responding to hurts."

What ever way your parents found or decided to give you your name, the ultimate person who gave you your name is God. Many youth today have never learned to accept themselves, and by rejecting their name (especially if it has a negative meaning), have greatly hindered their relationship with God and others. When a father calls his son by a negative expression like "good for nothing," his son will set out in bitterness to prove his father wrong. His name will influence the final outcome of his life's development.

In reality, most names can have a negative and positive meaning. That's why you have to go past the cultural meaning to understand the character definition of a name. By taking the cultural meaning of a name and applying study and perception to it, you can bring out rich facets of Godly character that God wants to see in your life. We can see a powerful example of this in the life of a man in the Bible called Moses. Pharaoh's daughter named him Moses, "…because I drew him out of the water." (Ex. 2:10) However it is important to note that she chose the *Egyptian* word for "Moses" rather than the Hebrew word, (sorry, we can't go into a deep study about this now!) but by using the Egyptian word for Moses, Pharaoh's daughter gave to her adopted son a royal heritage which would one day force him to choose between the treasures of Egypt and the affliction of God's people. His name gave him direction to find his purpose in life because first he was "drawn out" from the water, then God "drew him out" from the pleasures of Egypt, to later "draw out" the children of Israel from years of slavery and bondage.

You see, by learning how to translate your name into a proper understanding of God's purposes for your life, you will have a new motivation to live up to it glorifying God, as well as be constant reminder that you are "super" special in God's eyes and He calls you by name!

7. D.I.G (Delight in God)

My family and I live in Mexico and ever so often we have to make trips across the border. On one of those occasions, I was about twelve. I had saved up my money from the whole year, as usual, to be able to buy something at a favorite store when we crossed the border. I had this beautiful, small, light blue, leather wallet where I kept all my savings, it was my favorite color, but more importantly, my grandmother had passed this down to me as a heirloom, so I was quite proud of being able to have something "valuable" under my possession.

Finally the day came, I had saved up about $40, and was quite pleased with myself! I headed straight for that favorite store, and was soon in wonderland trying on clothes! If you're my type of a person, you know how easy it is to forget everything else around you when you're trying on clothes. I mean, the store walls could collapse around me and I wouldn't have realized it! Finally, after a few hours and piles of clothes, I picked out some beautiful pieces of clothing, took them to check out, and just as I was about to take out my long-saved money…it wasn't there! I had kept my wallet in my pocket but now it wasn't there! I must have laid it down while trying on clothes and forgot to pick it up again. So I raced back to the dressing rooms, barged into the room I had been in and frantically searched everywhere, but found nothing. One of the attendants must have cleaned out the piles of clothing and it was probably in there. I went to ask the people at the front desk, but never found it. Every penny of my savings was there! And what would grandma say about her wallet?! Oh, that was the most tragic suffering for this twelve-year-old! I cried and cried all night, and at that moment God said to me, "*Now* are you delighting in that wallet with that money?" No!

You see so many times we find ourselves *overly* delighting in things when we don't even think we are. God wants us to "search for Him as for hidden treasure" and delight and rely on Him and Him only and he will give you the desires of your heart.

As Psalms 37:4 says, "Delight yourself in the Lord and He will give you the desires of your heart."

I remember a time when there was the possibility that I go to England with some youth from another church. We were going to attend this international youth conference. We found out about this trip just about two months before and I had only ten dollars in my pocket. My parents told me that if it was God's will that I go, then He would provide and open all the doors for me to go. To make a very long story short, I'll just say that miraculously, He provided for the overall cost of the trip however, I still needed to consider costs for my trip from here, Monterrey, Mexico to Texas, where I would join the rest of the team of youth. The days went by and nothing happened, so I thought, "Well I probably wouldn't go because things seem "impossible." Then one morning, I think it was about one week before the rest of the team was departing for England, and the phone rang. It was a call from a friend of my parents saying that he had felt in his heart that God wanted him to send us a check (I like that man). At the time we didn't really think anything about it, but when we received it in the mail, can you believe it was the very same amount we needed for my round trip ticket to Texas! Not a dollar more or less. I remember thinking "Wow God! You really *are* there! You really *do* care about little me!" As it says in Psalms, it was like I was actually tasting and seeing that the Lord is good!

8. Be Attentive To His Process

One practical discipline that has been very important in my life in this area is keeping a journal. The difference between a journal and a diary is that, a diary is more like a book written by you about yourself, your personal thoughts, emotions, feelings, experiences, tragic moments, heartbreaks, etc. A journal is like a record of all that God has done in your life and the people He has used to mold character in you.

When I first started keeping journals, Mom had bought me one just as a normal "girly" thing to do. I didn't really know what to do or how to keep a journal, and I thought I had to write every day, so I started doing it. What normal nine-year-old girl, with a zillion more "important" things to do in her day, would last long writing in a journal? For me, it was like a ton of extra homework, so finally, even before ending my first journal book, I wrote, "OK, now I am going to stop and take a vacation from this journal stuff, goodbye forever!"

What a big mistake! So many awesome things happened that year, and I didn't take the time to write them down. Now I know better, I just write whenever I have an urge to write, or something great happens that I just have to write it down.

I think its good to keep a journal of all the things God does in your life, especially during your teen years. You know, the reason we now have the outstanding testimonies of two modern-day martyrs from Columbine, Cassie Bernal and Rachel Scott, is because of what they wrote in their journals. Truly the pen is mightier than the tongue.

When I first started keeping journals, I did it with the desire in my heart that I wanted to have something to leave in this world even after I'm gone that would remind the world that I was not just another human being passing through, I wanted to be remembered for something great.

But now as I think of it, my focus has changed some, I think it would be so wonderful after I grow old, publish these "books" for my grandkids to have as a record of the life of an ordinary girl with an extraordinary God.

It's so exciting because God is the author of these books, my journals, and each time it is like I'm starting a new chapter in my life. He's writing this new chapter about my life! This is history but it's *His*tory. This is one of the reasons I have been able to tell you so many stories from my personal life, I just go back and read my journals! And even more important than anything, is that I can look back on unpleasant situations, and really see what the Lord was trying to teach me then, and sometimes when I didn't learn the lesson the first time, it was like God just took me through the same thing all over again until I did learn! So I would encourage you to take time out of your "busy" life to listen to Him and be attentive to His process.

As a normal part of finding your purpose and fulfilling Gods calling for you, He will always take you through a time of refining and purification. A potter's vessel isn't complete and ready for use until after it has gone through the fire. If the vessel doesn't go want to go through the fire, it will forever stay contaminated and unstable. It needs the fire to strengthen, harden and give it firmness. He may bring persecution so you will cry out for more grace. Though it is not always a pleasant process, God is with you and as He reminds us in Isaiah 43:2 "When you pass through the waters I will be with you; and when you pass through the rivers, they will not sweep over you. When you walk through the fire, you will not be burned; the flames will not set you ablaze. For I am the Lord, your God."

Charles Spurgeon said, "The Refiner is never very far from the mouth of the furnace when His gold is in the fire."

9. Trust In His Faithfulness

"Though the fig tree does not bud and there are no grapes on the vines, though the olive crop fails and the fields produce no food, though there are no sheep in the pen and no cattle in the stalls, yet I will rejoice in the Lord, I will be joyful in God my Savior." -Habakkuk 3:17

Let's imagine you had a certain disease, (this is only imagination!) and the hospital called you up and told you that this particular disease is incurable. It so happened that modern technology had just invented a pill that could only keep you alive for the next twenty-four hours. You were glad to hear the news, but saddened to hear that they could only make *one* pill a day for you. You made long hard journey to the hospital every day to get your pill, and you depended on it because it was your last and only source of life.

That is just how God wants us to be with Him, He is our only source of spiritual life. Just how Adam and Eve died spiritually that day they disobeyed God's command, we will also die spiritually if we are not careful to rely on God on a daily basis, trust in His faithfulness, and recognize that, without His holding up this very universe, we would be nothing. God promises us that we can be safe and secure when we structure our life around that which is eternal and lasts forever. A wise man said, "When you have nothing left but God, then for the first time you become aware that God is enough."

I think if we had to summarize the whole Bible, its overall message could be said in these four words, "God is in Control." He knows every prayer that you've prayed and every tear that you cried, He has promised that His love will be with you, and you'll never be alone. He'll walk with you through the shadow of the valley of death and He will be your hiding place. Build your life upon The Rock, and storms *will* come, but the difference is that you *will* stand strong, in the face of adversary. You *can* have the victory!

"Thou tallest my wanderings: put thou my tears into thy bottle: are they not in thy book?" —Psalms 56:8 You are so special for God that He catches your every tear in His bottle and writes them down in His book!

Theodore Roosevelt once said, "Real success consists in doing one's duty well in the path where one's life is led." You will be successful when you live your lives at its maximum for God, and seek to honor Him in everyday in everything we do. Don't burn up the years of your youth, have high goals and standards now! Live it so you can look back later on in life and say, " I did something great with my life, I don't have any regrets."

Someone once said, "You don't need to know where you are going, provided you know whom you are following."

There is a story about a young man who grew up in a good, moral home with loving parents and a good family atmosphere. He had just become a Christian and was so excited with this new life God had given him, that all he wanted to do was serve Him and find his purpose in life. At a Bible study, another guy talked about how anyone who wanted to serve God could join a group that he worked with and serve God in any number of places around the world. To make a long story short, this guy joined the mission group. From the first day of being with the group, he heard about how God had a purpose and calling for his life and wanted to use him. In his heart he said, "Yes, one day I will do something great for God."

Many years passed and this young man did many great things for God. He traveled, preached, and explored many opportunities, looking for his "call". He reached out to many people in many nations of the world; he tried everyway he knew to find his destiny in God. Like a weary traveler in search of his destiny he had many great experiences, but none he could look back on and really say, "This is my calling and destiny in Christ."

In a moment of painful frustration after many years of dreams suppressed and hopes dashed, this guy asked the question of God, "What am I doing wrong? How have I missed Your calling? I see You releasing other people into their 'call' all the time, but I am still waiting. Where did I miss You?"

Then in the quiet of his spirit he heard the Spirit of God say, "My call to you and all My children is to be faithful…you be concerned with faithfully serving Me today, and let Me be concerned with your call."

You see, faithfulness is simply obeying God today. Maria Teresa said, "God hasn't called me to be successful. He's called me to be faithful."

Doing your part in the Kingdom of God is what counts. If it happens to be a world famous endeavor, that's great. If it's not, that's fine too. Has anyone ever heard the names of those mechanics who built the airplanes that were used to win World War 2? No. We only hear of the pilots who flew them, and yet that doesn't take one ounce of value away from the builders. They were both *extremely* important to accomplish what was accomplished! In the same way God has called some to live in the spotlight, and others backstage. But our attitude should be as Paul says in Philippians 3:14, "I press toward the mark for the prize of the high calling of God in Jesus Christ."

The God of the universe wants you to know that you are

important to Him and the direction of your life is critical to Him. God's not trying to hide His purpose from you, He wants to show you, He can't wait to begin! But...He want you to come to Him and lay down all *your* plans at His feet and with your whole heart say, "Here I am God, take my life, and do with it whatever you want. Show me what You want for my life, I want to be in the center of your will." Remember, we speak history, but God speaks destiny!

10

Acquiring a Hunger and Passion for Christ

"**O** God, you are my God, earnestly I seek you; my soul thirsts for you, in a dry and weary land where there is no water." -Psalms 63:1

There was once a young man who was searching everywhere because he wanted to know more about God. He decided he would go and ask another older, wise man who lived in the same village. After arriving to his house, he asked the old wise man his question, "How can I get to know more about God?" The old wise man said, "Come with me, let's take a walk to the river." So this younger man followed him, and after arriving at the river, the older man said, "Let's go down into the river." So they walked in until the water got about chest high. The older man took his hands and pushed the younger man under the water! He held him under a few seconds while the younger man struggled and struggled.

Then the old man brought him up from underwater, and the younger man, surprised, asked, "What were you doing to me?!" Then the old wise man asked him, "When you were under water, what was it that you wanted the most?" "Air!" he answered. Then the older man said, "When you get that desperate for more of God, is when you will be filled. But you have to really be hungry, you have to come desperate."

I think the wise man's words can relate to us because more than anything else in the whole world, we desperately need God. How desperate are you?

If you saw some kid lying on the side of the road and he's well dressed but he's looking real sick, and you say, "Kid, are you ok?" And he says, "No, I'm feeling very weak." And you say, "Well are you eating right?" And the kid says, "Well no, I haven't eaten for days but it's because I don't really feel like eating." And you say, "Kid, if you don't eat, you're going to die! Here, have a sandwich." He says, "But I don't really feel like eating."

When you go without food for a few meals, your body's digestive system automatically "shuts down" to where you won't feel hungry anymore. And if you let it stay 'shut down' for a few days or months, you'll eventually starve to death, and you may not even feel it. It's the same way with Christianity. In today's modern church we find multitudes of professing Christians suffering from spiritual malnutrition. Everything always seems to be going wrong in their life and you say, "Well hey, are you feeding on God's word *daily*?" They say, "Well I've got this problem and that problem and I'm just such a busy person that..." Oh come on! Susanna Wesley had *nineteen* children, and she still found one hour a day to meditate upon God and read his word. She had her priorities straight!

You could say, "Oh well I read the Bible every other day." So you go one hundred and eighty days a year without reading the Word?

Catherine Booth had already read the Bible through eight times by the time she was twelve years old! At our age, can't we do any better? (And I say this for myself too!)

Where is our zeal and outward evidence of your love for God?! Guys and girls it *has* to show! Webster's dictionary defines the word "zealous" as having a "passionate ardor in pursuit of something". It means "fervent in mind, wholly committed to cause, seeking or desiring eagerly, demonstrating a very warm interest in, vigorous, ardent, earnest, and intense." It is up to you to make your mind interested because your carnal flesh won't want anything to do with God. We have to learn to be more zealous for God!

Peter 2:2 says, "As newborn babes, desire the sincere milk of the word, that ye may grow thereby." Babies have an inbuilt instinct to scream for dear life if they don't drink. We are commanded to do the same. As a newborn Christian receives spiritual nutrition, he will grow, and his hunger and thirst for God and His righteousness will grow too. Just as an infant can't wait a week between feedings, so you cannot remain spiritually healthy by depending upon church services for all your spiritual nourishment. God's word is the spiritual food that will help you face life's difficulties.

I'm telling you, that if you are not hungering and thirsting after God, you're slowly starving to death! Get moving! Discipline yourself, that's all it takes. Hungering and thirsting for God doesn't always just explode like gasoline. Some morning it might be like a sweet, strawberry shortcake and you're really "delighting" in it. Other times it may be like a dry, milk-less granola you're chewing on just because you have to. Both ways, it is still good nourishment. Many times *I* don't feel like reading the Bible but I do it anyway because I don't go by feelings, I go by discipline. Join the army and see if that helps you! We are one body in the army of Christ and the basic principle is to discipline yourself into the "war manual" and *do* what it says!

James 1:22-25, tell us to "...not merely listen to the word, and so deceive yourselves. Do what it says. Anyone who listens to the word but does not do what it says is like a man who looks at his face in a mirror and, after looking at himself, goes away and immediately forgets what he looks like. But the man who looks intently into the perfect law that gives freedom, and continues to do this, not forgetting what he has heard, but doing it-he will be blessed in what he does." Every word and phrase of Scripture is a storehouse of rich wisdom and insight. God wants us to open these storehouses, enjoy the wealth they contain, and apply them to our lives. But we can't have an imbalance of head knowledge, we have to be committed to hearing *and* doing.

God tells us in Proverbs 2, "My son, if you will accept my words and store up my commands within you, turning your ear to wisdom and applying your heart to understanding, and if you call out for insight and cry aloud for understanding, and if you look for it as for silver and search for it as for hidden treasure, then you will understand the fear of the Lord and find the knowledge of God."

That word in the last verse "knowledge", is a key word of what we will find and its definition does not referring to head-knowledge, but instead supernatural revelations from God. That's when obedience steps in. God's prerequisites are that we "*accept* His words", "*store up* His commandments" (inside your heart, not inside your closet!), "turn your ear to wisdom", "*apply* your heart to understanding", and "*search* for it as for silver or hidden treasure", and *then* you will experience true revelations of God and He will make himself real to you. Remember that the most precious of rubies are never found near the surface. You have to dig deep, deep underground. The choice is up to you.

We talk a lot about the Christian life and our Christian walk with God. Yet we don't realize just how easy we let the secular world around us, rather than our faith, determine the routine of our lives, and it tends to set the pattern of our day. When we get up in the morning, what's the first thing we think of? Maybe a cup of hot tea or coffee, a shower, breakfast, and then its off to school or off to work. If we've got time, we'll spend some time praying or reading the Bible. That tends to be the first thing that slips away, if we "really don't have time". We wouldn't really think of going without breakfast or a shower, but we *would* think of going without prayer time. In Jesus' life, time with God really took priority over time in everything else. It even took priority over ministry time. There were times when Jesus just left the crowds in order to disappear up into the hills to pray. For those of you that are full-time in the Christian ministry, you know how easy it is to get caught up and overwhelmed by the sense of all the work there needs to be done. We have to realize that so many times when we get really busy, even doing good things like serving the Lord, our spiritual life is the first thing that lacks.

In Job 23: 12 he says, "I have esteemed the words of his mouth more than my necessary food." Did you catch that? "...more than my necessary food!" In the New International Version it says, "I have treasured the words of his mouth more than my daily bread."

Since the day I was born, my dad has gathered our family together for morning devotions, so his policy always is, "No Bible, no breakfast, no read, no feed."

Joshua 1:8 says that, "This book of the law shall not depart out of thy mouth; but thou shalt meditate therein day and night, that thou mayest observe to do according to all that is written therein: for then thou shalt make thy way prosperous, and then thou shalt have good success."

Right here is the secret to success! When we meditate and memorize the Bible, it is as if we are engrafting a tiny micro-chip of God's heart into ours, and the more we do this, the more security we will have in life because then we will start to see life's circumstances a little more from God's point of view. Meditation is "talking to the King, in the

King's own words."

A key element in Jesus' life is that he had a tremendous knowledge of the Scriptures. We need to make sure we get a good foundation and deep roots in the Scriptures so that when we're tempted as Jesus was out in the wilderness, He had Scripture right there, they kind of bounced off His tongue the moment the enemy came and tempted Him. Yet, the truth is, most of us don't know enough Scripture for that to be possible, and we can't be shielded from the temptations the enemy sends our way just because we don't have the kind of spiritual knowledge to make that possible. Make it your No.1 priority the development of your spiritual life. Your relationship with God should not be just an emotional illusion, but a life changing experience that lasts forever. So, for your own sake and for the sake of those around you who are still in their sins, discipline yourself to read and meditate on the Word.

When a newborn baby first starts to savor food, the first things the mother gives him is what he will hunger for and want more of, whether it be meat, fruits, vegetables, or candy.

Just like that, he will want more and more, and it all started by just one little taste. However, it is important to realize that it's so easy to contaminate ourselves with the wrong kind of "food."

One time I remember, I was at a restaurant with some friends, and the music that was playing was full of curse words. Here we were, just trying to get a bite to eat, and we had to tolerate hearing music full of profanity boomin' in our ears! We went up and talked to the manager about it and he apologized and changed the station. But that would have *never* happened unless somebody had gotten up and said, "I've had enough of this and I'm not tolerating anymore contamination!"

So many times we've compromised with sin, but God

didn't set you up to drink from a contaminated world, you're not immune to that! Be careful what your cup is full of. When there is a river with contaminated water, and you're trying to clean it up, it won't work for you to cleanse it by pouring in clean water. It will just get a little diluted that way. You have to clean and drain out all that contamination *first*, and *then* fill it up with purified water. So if you're going to get full and stay full of living water, you're going to have to drain out all that contaminated water.

Many times I think we get to comfortable at being in church and in His presence, that we loose that thirst for His presence. We have gotten so accustomed to having God's blessing over our lives that we forget what a life is without God, and how much greater things God has in store for us that we haven't yet realized or received.

We could get dry after a while too, unless we daily cry out to Him, "Lord, give me a new and fresh anointing from You so that my soul may never run dry."

11

Daniel: The Chronicle of a Faithful Man of God

In 586 B.C., King Nebuchadnezzar destroyed Jerusalem and carried away the remaining inhabitants of Judah to captivity in Babylon, the magnificent capital of the new empire. Before that, the Chaldeans controlled all of the Fertile Crescent including the Southern Kingdom of Judah. Of all the men an women of God in the Bible, one of my favorites is Daniel, he stands out to me as the perfect role model of God's will for the lives of all of us as young people.

Daniel was born during the middle of Josiah's reign, but after Josiah was killed in the battle against Egypt, the Southern Kingdom of Judah had returned to its evil ways. Nebuchadnezzar became king of Babylonia and to demonstrate his dominance, King Nebuchadnezzar took many of Jerusalem's wisest men and most beautiful women to Babylon as captives, Daniel was among this group. He became like an orphan, because he was taken captive to another kingdom without his family. He was young, probably around 16 or 17, but he was mature enough that even when totally taken from his parents he remained faithful in his convictions to their teachings and to God for the rest of his life. Daniel was a man of an incredible, unquestionable virtue, he is one of the few men in the Bible who was, "blameless in all ways..." Because "Daniel *purposed* in his heart not to defile himself..." —Daniel 1:8 One of his secrets to protecting his virtue was establishing Biblical convictions *before* being tested. It is really neat to notice how Daniel never pushed or tried to enforce these convictions on his peers but instead just lived them out himself, standing alone, and later God exalted him for it. I am convinced that we need to have this type of strong, firm conviction about our beliefs so that when the enemy comes to us with temptations, we with can stand firm, and not fall.

12

Six Things Leaders Look For In Youth —Taken from Daniel 1:4

One of the hardest areas of a church's work has always been their youth, and sadly today many churches are starting to compete with the world in order to get the attention and win the hearts of their youth. One time a pastor was talking to my Dad about the youth of their church because they felt they were failing in this area and their way of reaching them. They had no desire to come to any of the church meetings or even participate in their youth activities, and this pastor knew something had to be done. He consulted another youth pastor who apparently looked to be successfully with his large group of youth, and this is the advice the other youth pastor gave him, he said, "With youth you have to be very practical and go light with the Bible because they don't like much Bible preaching. Also, youth are all into fun and games so I suggest you get a soda fountain with plenty of free cokes they can fill up on, then you need to buy some games like pool tables, air hockey, soccer balls and basket hoops, oh, and you can't forget computer software with Internet. That will really attract them so they can all come and have their fun while at church!"

Sounds pretty exciting doesn't it? But if they walk away saying, "Well that was a great show and very interesting, but I wonder what it was all about..." then your bullet has just missed the target. Most of those things *are* very good and enjoyable, and if you wanted to have a special youth day celebration or turn your church into a some circus or theme park for public enjoyment, those things might belong.

However, this type of competing is wrong for the church to use for the purpose of drawing the crowds of youth to church, because once again we are using the world's method, with a "Christian" goal in reach. We have let Satan into our sanctuaries in our desperate efforts to attract teenagers and worldly adults. In John 12:32, Jesus said, "and if I be lifted up from the earth, I will draw all men unto me." Rather than lifting the name of our Lord with dignity and honor, we are debasing everything He stands for. And the type of Christians that it will produce will be poor quality, most of whom backslide, and the rest need an extravagant church with plenty of activities and good music or they'll slip back into the world where their heart is. But if we want to see genuine, broken, contrite, repentant conversions to Jesus Christ, then we must seek anointing from God.

As George Whitefield said, "That is the reason we have so many "mushroom converts", they spring up overnight and then disappear."

Many times what we want is not always what we need. Even if we tried using these "control techniques", they wouldn't work with good, lasting fruit because these teens already *have* enough of all this outside the church and in the world, and even plenty more of it! Getting together a group of youth is not that hard of a task really, there are already "youth-groups" at schools, parties, discos, etc.

Now days we get a lot of entertainment but not enough discipleship. If you want to have much more than just quantity in youth, but also a quality of life that reflects a deep personal relationship with their Creator that surpasses anything else they could ever learn in the world, I think we have to start scraping a little deeper than the surface. You have to go deeper into their needs, looking deeper than their outward popularity and "happiness-mask" and start to realize that deep inside their hearts there is a cry for a sense of belonging, genuine love, acceptance, something more and different that the world can't give.

People will respond to that, and people will be attracted to come just because they have a passion and desire and they want to know and grow and learn and get what they're searching for. I suggest you raise up youth who are wholly committed to God and passionate for Him and let them preach and teach. Let them be the "main attraction." Because there is something really incredible that happens when one of your peers gets up to preach and teach.

John Wycliffe said, "Get on fire for God and people will come from miles around just to watch you burn!"

No. 1 Physical Appearance

"Then the king ordered Ashpenaz, chief of his court officials, to bring in some of the Israelites...young men without any physical defect, handsome..." —Daniel 1:4

I have to start out by saying this is a rather difficult subject to talk about because opinions on "physical appearance" is something most people today differ in. But I included this in one of seven things leaders look for in youth because such a small thing is actually very important if the king of Babylon had it as one of the seven requirements for those who entered his courts, and God wanted it to be included in the Bible.

Take a second and imagine you are walking down the street and you walk by a guy, all dressed up, from head to toe, in red and white Chicago Bulls. Obviously he's a Bulls fanatic wouldn't you think? But what made us think that? Did we have to talk to him about it? No. We could tell just by looking at him. Even without opening his mouth, his outward image was communicating a message.

One time there was a guy and a girl that had started coming to the youth group. They came from a rough background, their parents were divorced and they had gotten involved in many things, wrong friends, drugs, etc., so as you can imagine, they had piercings everywhere (in fact they had so many, if they took them out it could look like Swiss cheese!), black makeup, freaky hair, T-shirts with skulls, and different things like that. After I saw them at church, I went up to talk to them and get to know them, I got their phone number and became their friend. They got saved and started coming and meeting the other youth at the church. We just loved them and accepted them with unconditional love and as time passed, soon I noticed they had taken out all of their piercings, and their whole way of being changed. Did we say anything to them about their appearance? Not one word. No one had to. Maybe God did. And I can promise you that people will obey the voice of God when *He* wants to tell them something, more than anyone else trying to correct them. You say, "But how can they know how to hear God?" Don't you think God can get through to His own creation no matter how disconnected we are?

Today, they are some of the most influential youth in the church and they have been the ones to bring their unsaved friends to Christ which now make up over half of the whole youth group into the church.

I have no right to tell you what you should or shouldn't do. All I want to say is that wherever we go, whatever we are doing, our appearance *is* a very important part of our presentation, that is why when the king ordered his officials to look for some young men to be brought in to the kings courts, he specifically said these points which we are talking about. And this was No. 1 on his list! Remember, you never get a second chance for a better first impression!

"For ye are bought with a price: therefore glorify God in your body, and in your spirit, which are God's." -1 Corinthians 6:20 KJV

God's Word says that we are temples of the Holy Spirit. Even "Christian" tattoos and piercings are as if you have taken paint into your temple and thrown it all over the walls. Don't tear down your temple and build a Pizza Hut!

Notice in Israel's rebellion of Exodus Chapter 32, that the people "broke off their golden earrings," which speaks of some sort of bondage to Egypt.

A good etiquette book I read said, "It is hardly necessary to remind the reader that dress, though often considered a trifling matter, is one of considerable importance, for a man's personal appearance is a sort of "index and obscure prologue" to the character. Lord Chesterfield has said, "I cannot help forming some opinion of a man's sense and character from his dress." Besides, the appearance of a well-dressed man commands a certain degree of respect, which would never be shown to a sloven. As Shakespeare has written, "The world is still deceived by ornament;" and there are those who associate fine clothes with dine people so strongly, that they do not trouble themselves to ascertain whether the wearers are worthy of respect, as others from their opinions of books by the gilding of the leaves and beauty of the binding."

Even though God looks at your heart and knows your motives, man doesn't. Man looks at the *outward* appearance and they will judge you by how they see you on the outward. Not that this is good or anything, but that's why we should be even more careful that we protect Christ's reputation by not bringing any unnecessary reproach on ourselves, because of our outward appearance. Remember that things that maybe don't affect you, can be a distraction to the attention of others away from your spirit, away from Jesus himself, and your countenance, the real you! We are not to be conformed to this world, I repeat it again, we are not trying to get as close to the edge as possible, without crossing the line, but instead be as far away as possible from the edge, and get as close as we can to being more like Jesus! Our appearance is very important because it reflects what we feel in our heart. The Jesus I know sets you free from bondage so you don't have to wear it on your body and show it in your actions!

You could say, "Well, it's only "body art." As an ex-tattoo artist once told me, "Your body is clearly the temple of the Holy Spirit and God has only *loaned* it to you to live in during your earthly stay. But when you get to Heaven, and He asks you, "What did you do to this body I loaned you to take care of?" What would you answer Him? Let us do our best to serve God with all the dignity and honor He deserves!"

No. 2 A Joyful and Enthusiastic Countenance

"The light of the eyes rejoiceth the heart: and a good report maketh the bones fat." -Proverbs 15:30

Having a joyful enthusiastic countenance is a key element to being an energy giver, and there is nothing I love more, than to be around enthusiastic, energy-giving people! I have also seen it in the lives of friends that are still unsaved. When they talk about meeting a Christian that they really got along well with, they always add, "And she always seems so happy." This is a key element to reaching people

Six Things Leaders Look For In Youth

with the gospel because society is attracted to excited joyful passionate people!

Did you know that just by the expression on your face you are conveying a message. Having a joyful countenance isn't something that's based on feelings. A smile doesn't just mean, "I'm happy." It can also communicate just the fact that, "You are special in God's eyes."

A teacher in New York decided to honor each of her seniors in school by telling them the difference each made. She called each student to the front of the class and then she presented each of them with a blue ribbon imprinted in gold letters, which read, "Who I Am Makes a Difference". Afterwards, the teacher decided to do a class project to see what kind of impact praise and recognition would have on a community. She gave each of the students three more ribbons and instructed them to go out and use them to praise others with and then have those people praise others with it. Then come back and give their reports about what happened. One of the boys had given it to his boss at work. That night, his boss then took it home to his teenage son, with these words, "As I was driving home tonight, I started thinking, my days are really hectic and when I come home I don't pay a lot of attention to you. Sometimes I yell at you for not getting good enough grades in school and for your bedroom being a mess, but somehow tonight, I just wanted to let you know that you do make a big difference to me. Besides mother, you are the most important person in my life. You're a great kid and I love you!"

The startled teen started to sob and sob, and he couldn't stop crying. He looked up at his father and said through his tears, "Dad, earlier tonight I sat in my room and wrote a letter to you and Mom explaining why I had killed myself, and asking you to forgive me. I was going to commit suicide tonight after you were asleep. I just didn't think that you cared at all. Now I don't think I'll need it after all." That boss went back to work a changed man. You never know what kind of difference a little encouragement can make to a person.

Who you are makes a difference in this world and a simple smile of yours will be sure to bring happiness into the life of someone else, even if they may not like you or you may not even know them. Someone once said, a candle looses nothing by lighting another candle. The more effective your witness is, and the more you evangelize and share with the people around you, it will automatically rejuvenate you and renew the glow on your countenance and inwardly give you a new strength. Not to mention a smile is an inexpensive way to improve your looks!

No. 3 Youth Having A Teachable Spirit

"...young men...showing aptitude for every kind of learning." -Daniel 1:4

It was on the night of April 14, 1912, the world famous British luxury liner called "Titanic", sank in the icy, Atlantic Ocean, carrying with it the lives of one thousand, five hundred and twenty-two men women and children to watery graves. Being over one hundred and ten feet tall and nearly nine hundred feet long, the "Titanic" nicknamed the "Millionaires Special", was one of the largest, fastest and most opulent ships the world had ever seen. Its designers and builders boasted that "God himself could not sink the ship".

"The pride of your heart had decieved you, you who live in the clefts of the rocks and make your home on the heights, you who say to yourself, 'Who can bring me down to the ground?' Though you soar like the eagle and make your nest among the stars, from there I will bring you down, declares the Lord." —Obadiah 1:3

Six Things Leaders Look For In Youth

Pride is a subtle thing. A few years ago I was quickly walking into a grocery store when suddenly I came to an abrupt stop. I had walked straight into the automatic glass doors! They had opened too late! (dumb blond!) I could tell that the guard standing close by had seen it all and was trying to keep his laughter bottle up. Did I give thought to the pain coming from a "swollen" forehead? No! I just turned to the guard and gave him a "cheesy Christian grin" like, "I meant to do that!"

The Bible says God hates pride. It is a sin that will stop multitudes from entering the Kingdom of Heaven. Pride destroys families. It stops a husband or wife from admitting that they are wrong. They would rather break up a family and keep their pride, than humble themselves and be reconciled. As young teenagers, we have to keep reminding ourselves, we aren't natural born computers with all the information already built in, we have to learn it all, and that's where humility and obedience to higher authorities comes in.

There is also the story of a Greek hero named Phidias and the statue of the god which he had carved. After he had finished it, he had chiseled in the corner, in small letters, the word "Phidias", and it was objected that the statue could not be worshipped as a god, nor considered sacred, while it bore the sculpture's name. It was even seriously questioned whether Phidias should not be stoned to death because he had so desecrated the statue. How could he dare, they asked, to put his own name on the image of a god?

So some of us are very apt to want to put our little names down at the bottom of any work which we have done for God, that we might be remembered, whereas we ought rather upbraid ourselves for wishing to have any credit of that which God enables us to do.

Do you wish you had more liberty and independence? The typical mindset of our day is,

"It's my life, and I'm going to make my own decisions." And many times by nature we tend to resent authority. We have to remember one thing: even adults need guidance. As we grow and mature our authority changes from, "You have to do this and you can't do that" to "This is the best way." We shouldn't resent authority because God placed it over us to provide, protect, instruct, and correct us so we will be more like that person that God want us to be. Our authorities are there standing by us to say, "Let me help you, I just want the best for your life."

Galatians 5:13 says that "you have been called unto liberty; only use not liberty for an occasion to the flesh, but by love, serve one another." Many times our concept of authority is that we will have more liberty when we get out from underneath it, the truth is just the opposite. We will gain independence by our inward harmony and obedience to the authority He has already placed over us. We already talked about this earlier but I want to repeat that one of the qualities of an ambassador is that he will enjoy the guaranteed protection of his government *only* as he stays under their authority.

Jesus Christ shows us the ultimate and greatest example in obedience when He "humbled himself and became obedient unto death, even the death of the cross." -Philippians 2:7-8

No. 4 Youth Who Are Mature and Skillful In Wisdom

"...young men...well informed, quick to understand..." —Daniel 1:4

When I was about eight years old, I remember playing hide-and-seek with some friends.

When it came time for the searching part, the other twelve year old girl who was the one looking for us, said,

"Oh, you guys are acting so immature!" I wasn't sure what that big word was and now that I think of it, it was probably just so that we would come out faster! So at that time I guessed it had to do with some way you are acting.

What really is maturity? I ask myself. Webster's dictionary defines it as "something or someone complete, prepared, and ready."

Proverbs 1:8-9 says, "Listen, my son, to your father's instruction and do not forsake your mother's teaching. They will be like a garland to grace your head and a chain to adorn your neck."

A garland is like a crown, and when someone is wearing some chain around their neck, or something on their head, it is one of the first things others will see on him. Am I right? It works the same way with maturity. Anyone can act very educated, proper, or simply be a nice person, but does that mean he is mature? Maturity is something that everyone will see in a person, something that is visible, even before that person has to even open his mouth to say one word. Because maturity is something that shines from our inward character out, we need to put into practice the light we have from God's word, and let Him work more Godly character in us through our circumstances and people around us.

A true leader is seen in the lives of his wife and children. There are so many great preachers, and now even more, that are preaching, teaching and winning souls all over the world, but their own wives and children are lost. I remember one pastor who said, "Well, God has called me to preach not to occupy myself with my family." And I started thinking…What was the first thing God entrusted him *before* his ministry? His family.

For all you who are sons or daughters of someone in the ministry, you have the ability to greatly encourage, strengthen, and lift up your parents ministry by being mature young guys and girls. I have heard of many pastors who have had to step down from the ministry, because of some things their sons and daughters did. So we have a greater potential than we realize.

So I encourage you and lay it before you as a challenge, set apart a quiet time to be by yourself with God to search for His perfect will for your life, instead of just maturing with what you hear at church or other meetings.

Ecclesiastes 12:1 says, "Remember your Creator in the days of your youth, before the days of trouble come and the years will approach when you will say, "I have no pleasure in them." This word "youth" translated to the original Greek is *'bios'* and in this scripture it means "ones present state of existence." So actually it applies to all of us from all ages, in our lives now. God's desire for us is that we grow every day more mature in him so that "Then we will no longer be infants, tossed back and forth by the waves, and blown here and there by every wind..." -Ephesians 4:14

Proverbs 10:21 says, "The lips of the righteous feed many: but fools die for want of wisdom." You can read it in on the news, magazines, Internet, etc., fools actually *do* die for lack of wisdom. Proverbs 16: 16 says, "How much better is it to get wisdom than gold! and to get understanding rather to be chosen than silver!" Gold and silver is something that comes and goes, it just rotates in quantities! But wisdom and understanding are priceless! It is like a thermometer, you can never get to the point where you have *enough* wisdom and understanding.

For the last three-hundred or three hundred-fifty years, our thinking has become dominated by a scientific worldview. Those scientific pioneers like Newton, Kepler, Galileo, Boyle, Maxwell, Kelvin, Pasteur, Faraday, etc., all these great thinkers came up with fantastic equations to say, "This is how our world works." Not only did they do that, but also they could prove it through some of their machines and inventions. "If you do this, this, and that, a light bulb will spark into a light." "Do this type of stuff and you will get a car moving, eventually." They began to construct a whole world which they believed with logic. So this idea began to dominate and still dominates today's education. We're trained to believe that for everything there's a right answer. Big words, simple ideas. The world out there is logical, explainable, and understandable, and if we as human beings would just get that science right, then we would have an even greater potential impact the world in an even greater way. All the top world advisors have been great thinkers and overflowing in knowledge, but our bonus is... that we as Christians have supernatural wisdom from above to go with it.

In Psalms 119:97-101, David expresses his heart to God as he says, "O how I love thy law! It is my meditation all the day. Thou through thy commandments hast made me wiser than mine enemies...I have more understanding than all my teachers: for thy testimonies are my meditation. I understand more than the ancients, because I keep thy precepts."

When we apply God's law to our lives we will He promises to give us wisdom and knowledge that surpasses any human ability. Our God is the God of all knowledge and there is yet much in our world we do not understand. Yet, as He gives us the opportunity, we should constantly seek a greater understanding, not for our own glory but for a greater knowledge of Him.

No. 5 Youth having the Courage to stand alone under peer pressure and stress

"...young men...qualified to serve in the kings palace."
-Daniel 1:4

Sparkling as it crashes against boulders along its banks, the river cascades down toward the sea. The current grabs, pushes and tugs at leaves and logs, carrying them along for the ride. Here and there a sportsman in a kayak, going with the flow. Gravity pulls the water, and the river's force is what pulls the rest...downward. Suddenly, a silver missile breaks the surface and darts upstream, and then another, and another. Oblivious to the swirling opposition of the white waters, these salmon strive to swim against the strong current. They must go upstream and nothing will stop them from reaching their destination.

Someone once said, "To get nowhere follow the crowd." There are only a few people on this earth that have the courage with stand alone and stay firm under pressure and stress. It is a characteristic that will grow in us when it becomes a continual practice every time pressures come in our everyday life.

Once I read the story of a man that had a passion for winning souls, and everywhere he went, he was sharing with everyone about Jesus. No one got saved. He went on like this for over ninety years! Still no one got saved. At times he got very discouraged, but he kept right on, sharing with everyone about Jesus. In the eyes of other preachers, he could be seen as a failure and ineffective as an evangelist, because he never had a single convert. Then one day God spoke to him about a coming disaster on the earth, and God instructed him build a structure, which would save him, his family, and some other inhabitants of the earth. Because he had an obedient and hearing heart to the voice of the Lord, he and his whole family were saved. He may not have had one single convert, but he, along with his family made a lasting impact on all the people who surrounded them. They stood alone under peer pressure and stress. They were the only family in the whole nation who didn't conform or be influenced by the world. He may not have saved the world, but he saved his family, which is the first and most valuable of all possessions God entrusted him. Who was this man? If

Six Things Leaders Look For In Youth

you said Noah, you guessed it! Have you ever thought of the fact that in those days, there had never once fallen a drop of rain on the earth? He had no clue what this thing called "rain" was, and why God was telling him to build a boat to save himself! It could have been even harder because this was a task that would take him over one hundred years to complete, practically the rest of his life! Nevertheless, he stood alone with his family, amid the mocking and insults of their friends and neighbors.

To stand alone is one of the most important things we can learn during our teen years. When you stand alone, in the face of temptation, on a certain conviction or standard, you may get the "Boo/Hooray reaction," and your *acquaintances* may laugh at you, call you names, mock at you, and criticize you, but your *true* friends won't. They will respect you despite your beliefs.

But what does it mean to "stand alone?" It means that we are different from the secular world around us in the values and the standards we have. The hardest part of standing alone, is just *that*, sometimes you do have to stand alone. There are many Bible heroes we learned about as little kids in Sunday school who we can take an example after when they stood alone. One of them is Esther. I'm sure you know the story, she really stood alone, even when her life was at risk.

Then there's Joseph. He is a great example of standing alone because he had the courage to stand strong, say "no", and run from temptation. Even when it cost him his freedom, position in government, level of respect and a few years in prison, because he chose to do the right thing. I think he is one of the most outstanding and encouraging characters in the whole Bible because he is one of the few persons who was able to maintain spiritually stable in the highest point of success as well as in the midst of trouble.

"Joseph is a fruitful vine, a fruitful vine near a spring,

whose branches climb over a wall. With bitterness archers attacked him; they shot at him with hostility. But his bow remained steady, his strong arms stayed limber...because of the Shepherd, the Rock of Israel." -Genesis 49:22-25

In a world that loves sin, those who stand for righteousness will suffer. They may receive a frown from the world, but they will have the smile from God. Romans 16:19 says, "...but yet I would have you wise unto that which is good, and simple concerning evil."

In other words, you don't have to know the wrong to know it's wrong. Know the right so well, that you can be sure you'll know when a wrong is wrong.

The way the U.S. federal agents train their officers to recognize counterfeit bills is to have them study the genuine article. When they see the false, the spot it immediately because their eye is trained to know the right thing.

"Beloved, believe not every spirit, but try the spirits whether they are of God: because many false prophets are gone out into the world..." —1 John 4:1

In the same way, we are not to know evil with our minds, but instead discern it with our spirits. William Penn said, "Right is right, even if everyone is against it, and wrong is wrong even if everyone is for it."

No. 6 Youth Who Really Walk Their Talk

In 1945 there was a young man called Dietrich Bonhoffer who was imprisoned at Flossenburg concentration camp in Germany. He was sentenced to be killed for joining a bomb plot to kill Hitler, just before the war ended. Dietrich earned a reputation as a brilliant theologian and even until his death, he wrote many letters from prison. In one of them he was writing to a friend and he said, "What is increasingly taking me up is, what does it mean to be a

Six Things Leaders Look For In Youth

Christian today? I want to know what religion-less Christianity would look like in our world."

Anymore, everyone and anyone call themselves a Christian just like I can say I'm Guatemalan but don't really look it. Many times we as Christians look like those famous stars who advertise products and you just know they don't even use what they're advertising! We call ourselves Christians because we follow Christ, but now it's time to change and not just follow, but strive for Christ's character. As we study more in depth of the Bible, we will find out that these first century believers didn't just act like Christians- they *were* Christ-like. Remember, with God it *is* possible! You can learn to talk like a Christian, and act like a Christian, and yet *not* be a truly transformed, born again "Christian" at all—just as I can try to speak German, act German, eat German food, and still be a Spanish-born American at heart! (I was originally born in Guatemala).

What I'm trying to say with this is, your "cosmetic" presentation does not always evidence who you are on the inside. And the sad, scary part is that at some point your outward mask will wear thin, and who you are will really begin to leak out. (Actually this breakdown usually happens when under pressure, and then you don't leak out—you explode!)

Leo Tolstoy searched for a meaning to life that would not be destroyed beyond the grave and he earnestly looked for the answer in the lives of believers around him and he said, "No rationalization could convince me of the truth of their faith, though one thing might have: actions proving that these people held the key to the meaning of life that would eliminate in them the fear of poverty, sickness, and death that haunted me."

Hypocrites may show up at a church building every Sunday, but there are no hypocrites in the Church (Christ's body). Hypocrite comes from the Greek word for "actor", or pretender. Hypocrisy is "the practice of professing beliefs, feelings, or virtues that one does not hold." The Church is made up of true believers; hypocrites are "pretenders" who sit among God's people. God knows those who love Him, and the Bible warns that He will sort out the true from the false on the Day of Judgment.

Arthur R. Adams said, "Don't stay away from church because there are so many hypocrites. There's always room for one more."

But you don't have to go to church to find a hypocrite. A hypocrite is he who says "I believe I God" when his lifestyle shows it is nothing but empty words. Hypocrisy is having "In God We Trust" on our money, and yet use His Holy name to curse. (Adolf Hitler's name wasn't even despised enough to be used as a curse word! Yet men blaspheme the name of the God who gave them life.) Hypocrites sing "God bless America", and then throw out prayer and the Ten Commandments from the schools. Hypocrisy is a society that says it cares for children, yet murders millions in the womb.

If the whole world hates a hypocrite, what must *God* think of him? A wise preacher said, "If the hypocrite so offends you, you won't want to spend eternity in Hell with him would you?

This is such an important aspect for our lives because we can have all the head-knowledge we want, but if we don't balance it out with virtue, and really live it, then we will become more destructive to those around us than a blessing.

Many times I'll be talking to an unsaved person and their first expression and impression about a Christian is: "Yeah I have Christian friends but they sure don't live it!"

The Christian life *is* impossible to live! That's why you need the power behind it, which is the power of the Holy Spirit. When Jesus back to heaven to prepare a place for you and me, He gave us the Holy Spirit to empower us to truly live the Christian life. One of the reasons we see lots of people

Six Things Leaders Look For In Youth

who claim to be Christians but don't live it (and I use to be one of them) is because they are not fully walking in the power of the Holy Spirit. Commit yourself to walk your talk and live your whole life for Jesus.

I love the historical example of Count Ludwig Nicholas von Zinzendorf of the eighteenth century. When he was in the university he formed a type of a cell group which they called the, "Society of the Grain of Mustard". He and several others who were also in it, made a promise, which was a lifetime vow and they had it engraved on a ring. This vow was to three things: to be forever true to Christ, to be kind to all people, and to take the gospel to the end of the earth. When he came home from the university, he found that the landlord allowed a community of refugees to build their village on his land. That's when he remembered the ring on his finger and that he vowed to be kind to all people. So he let them stay and live on his land even though they were peasants. Years later, when the Holy Spirit fell, and revival came and the hundred years' prayer meeting began in August 30 of 1727, Zinzendorf could not help but say, "We will be true to Christ by taking the gospel to the ends of the earth because I have this vow written on the ring of my finger that out of this chaotic, anti-God world, which we live in today, we will take the good news of Jesus Christ to the West Indian Slavs. That influence later converted John Wesley and inspired William Carey, and shook the very world we live in."

1 John 3:18 reminds us, "...let us not love in word, neither in tongue; but in deed and in truth."

Jesus said that the greatest commandment of all is Love. Joshua Harris says in his book, "I Kissed Dating Goodbye," "The world shows us a huge screen where projected are images of passion and romance, and as we observe it the world *tells* us: "This is love". But God takes us to the foot of a piece of wood where hung on it is the bleeding body of a man, and *shows* us "*This* is love".

Love God with *all* your heart don't worry about anything else, get busy just loving people everywhere because that is the one most important thing this world needs and is looking for everywhere, without really *knowing* about what they're looking for. Genuine love is a love that is sustained amid distractions. Show God's love and you will change your generation. Show God's love in your church and people will be drawn to it, it will never lack new converts, and it will never grow cold because it will never lack the presence of God!

At a certain college they were having a class on different religions. After discussing different religions and the characteristics of their principles, doctrines and teachings, one student stood up and said, "What might a Christian look like?" The teacher responded, "The actual characteristics are hard to define or point out, but you see that young man walking down the hall? You're looking at a true Christian."

Wouldn't you like for people to say that about you? I sure would!

Live the quality of life that reflects Jesus. Don't just *talk* the quality of life that reflects Jesus. Live it. I think this is very important because otherwise we end up with people thinking that if they can just learn to listen to some new music and wear some new clothes, somehow the kingdom of God will forcefully advance, but it's just not the issue.

In John 13:35, Jesus says, "A new commandment I give unto you, That ye love one another; as I have loved you, that ye also love one another. *By this shall all men know that ye are my disciples*, if ye have love one for another." (My italics)

Genuine love. This is where the rubber meets the road. This is where it all boils down to what real Christianity is all about.

13

Satan's No. 1 Most Effective Strategy of Attack: Relationships

There was a time in Susanna Wesley's life when she and her husband got into an argument over a political matter because she thought that William the 3rd, Prince of Orange, was the rightful heir to the throne of England at the time. However her husband Samuel was convinced that King William should be the next King. Susanna describes the incident in a letter she later wrote to a friend of hers saying, "He immediately kneeled down and imprecated divine Vengeance upon himself and all his posterity if he ever touched me or came into bed with me before I had begged God's pardon and his, for not saying "Amen" to the prayer for the king." Having sworn a vow, Samuel Wesley strode into his study, packed his saddlebags, and headed for the outside door. He mounted his horse and galloped away. He was convinced he would never change his mind.

After the death of King William and many months of

God working in their hearts, they were brought to reconciliation. I wanted to use this story to illustrate this point because more than just being a normal disagreement they had, Satan was trying his hardest to destroy their marriage and family because he knew that if not, right after that one of the greatest history makers of all time was to be born, John Wesley.

Just as Jesus Christ was the same yesterday, today and forever, Satan is also the same yesterday, and today (but not forever!) and his favorite tactics are still to kill, steal, destroy, deceive, and distract us from our ultimate goal: To be more like Jesus.

Think of it, in the world we live in today, we have taller buildings and wider streets, but we are more narrow minded and have shorter tempers. We spend more, but enjoy less. We have bigger houses but smaller families, We have more commitments but less time. We have multiplied our possessions, and have reduced our values. We talk a lot, love very little, and hate too much. We have already taken man to the moon and back, but we still have difficulty going next door to tell our neighbors about Jesus. We have conquered the outer space but not yet the inward space. We have higher income but less moral and more divorce. We live in a world with more freedom, but less happiness. We live in nicer houses, but of broken homes.

I believe that one of the greatest but subtle tactics the devil uses to try to steal, kill and destroy us as Christians is through relationships. In the following four chapters we will talk about four powerful areas such as drugs, gossip, dating and friendships that the enemy tries to use to attack us as youth.

14

Garbiology

"**A**nd the tongue is a fire a world of iniquity: so is the tongue among our members that it defileth whole body, and setteth on fire the course of nature; and it is set on fire of hell." -James 3:6

Cutting, burning, piercing, venomous, scathing words, slanderous reports, galling statements, and angry retorts, this are just a few of all the "flaming missiles" and garbage that can pour out of one of the smallest, most harmless member of our body. The tongue. "Friendly fire" is the army's way of saying that they killed their own troops. It's an absurd expression. There is nothing "friendly" about being shot by your own side. "Stupid", "tragic", "betrayal" are far more applicable. Whatever it's called, to kill someone in your own army is to do the work of the enemy. Satan's ultimate power of destruction is released when he uses Christians to attack other Christians.

How many times have you been in the kind of a "betrayal" where your opponent is a friend? From those whom you trusted and least suspected would be the source of verbal attack. I think those are some of the most hurtful cases. It happened to David too, he said, "For it was not an enemy that reproached me; then I could have borne it neither was it be that hated me that did magnify himself against me...but it was thou, a man mine equal, my guide and mine acquaintance. We took sweet counsel together, and walked unto the house of God in company... The words of his mouth were smoother than butter, but war was in his heart: his words were softer that oil yet were they drawn swords" —Psalm 55: 12-14,20

This happened more than once because again he says, "Yea, mine own familiar friend, in whom I trusted, which did eat of my bread, hath lifted up his heel against me." —Psalm 41:9

And again he cries, "Hide me from the secret counsel of the wicked: from the insurrection of the workers of iniquity: Who whet their tongue like a sword, and bend their bows to shoot their arrows, even bitter words: That they may shoot in secret at the perfect suddenly do they shoot at him, and fear not" —Psalms 64:2-4

You know, in most cases of verbal attacks between friends, it's because we ourselves are also guilty of doing the same thing to others behind their backs. We are the ones who will end up getting burned and pretty soon we become polluted and contaminated "garbage collectors", or in a nicer way of saying it "offense collectors".

Webster's dictionary defines gossip as: To prate; to chat; or to run about from place to place collecting and telling idle tales. It is telling something negative to someone who is not part of the problem or the solution.

Matthew 12:36-37 warns us by saying, "But I say to you to you that for every idle word men shall speak, they will give account of it in the day of judgment. For by your words you will be justified, and by your words you will be condemned."

The Greek translation of the word here "idle" is "*argos*" meaning inactive, unemployed, useless, barren. Something that is inactive is useless, and it starts rotting after a while and doesn't serve for anything. That's how our words become if we don't be careful. Gossip stems from the root cause of discontent, jealousy, and anger. So we need to always ask ourselves these questions before: will it be of "grace" unto the hearer, will it edify him, give him knowledge, encourage him? Or will it be more like "rottenness in his bones?"

I think this is a very important issue because gossip is also involved in three of the seven things the Lord hates. "There are six things the Lord hates, seven that are detestable to him: ...a lying tongue...a false witness who pours out lies and a man who stirs up dissension among brothers." -Proverbs 6:16-19

I'm sure you've heard the rhyme, "Sticks and stones may break my bones, but words will never hurt me." Yeah right! Words do more than hurt, they leave deep wounds and destructive infections which can bring about painful spiritual and physical death, when they are not resolved. When poisonous word are spoken they can be quickly spread by those who hear them, affecting the lives and decisions of many other people. Those who contaminate others with defiling words fall into three categories: those who have a root of bitterness (Hebrews 12:15); those who are talebearers (Proverbs 18:8); and those who subvert their listeners with false doctrine (2 Timothy 2:14-17).

Proverbs 25:18 says, "A man who bears false witness against his neighbor is like a club, a sword, and a sharp arrow." In other words he is a pain and danger to those around him.

Luke 24:10-11 tells us about when Mary Magdalene, Joanna, Mary the mother of James, and some other women told the apostles that Jesus had risen. It says, "And their words seemed to them like idle tales, and they did not believe them." Why? The word used here for "idle tales" in Greek is translated "leros" meaning "an incredible story". Could it be that maybe these women, in the past, spoke "idle words" and therefore now when it was something of truth no one believed them. We have to realize that gossiping doesn't only refer to murmuring or telling another person something wrong about someone else, it is also referring to consciously or unconsciously telling something but also adding things to make it more "incredible." How many of us are guilty of this?! How many times does your conversation boast about yourself?" (and I ask myself this question too). This is already something that has become acceptable and normal in our culture today, especially for girls.

One of my favorite chapters of the Bible is James 3 and I have made it my goal to read through it every day to remind me to watch my tongue. At the end of the day, I look back on its events and think what words I shouldn't have spoken so that the next day I can try to do better.

"You, then, why do you judge your brother? Or why do you look down on your brother? For we will all stand before God's judgment seat." —Romans 14:10

Matthew 18:15 says that when we have a problem with someone else, we are supposed to go to…him! *Not* everyone else in the place and take up votes to see who is on our side of the fight! We are supposed try to go talk with that person with all humility, recognizing and asking forgiveness, and work it out between the two.

On the Christian video series called the "Veggie Tales" there is an episode called the "Rumor Weed" which is about gossip. If you've seen the show, you know that the weed started out small with a tiny rumor, but then grew and grew until it was a massive, monster-sized root that grew underground. An interesting thing I saw there was that in the end of the story, no one could stop the "rumor weed" from destroying everything in its path, except one person. The one who started the rumor. And that's the truth. If we have started the rumor, we are the only ones who can stop it from spreading by rectifying it and telling the truth. So don't be a "garbiologist!" *You* have to empty out your own garbage!

In Bible days, many times God used leprosy as a punishment for gossip. I'm thinking, how much gossiping would there be around today if that was still the case?

"Curse not the king, no not in thy thought; and curse not the rich man in thy bed chamber: for a bird of the air shall carry the voice, and that which hath wings shall tell the matter." —Ecclesiastes 10:20

As I have already said, the best neutralizer of false statements is the truth. When the wicked men of the city tried to verbally destroy the work in the city that Nehemiah was doing, he answered and said, "...There are no such things done as thou sayest, but thou feignest them out of thine own heart." Nehemiah 6:8

Forgiveness is an important element for conquering gossip because cutting words can cause a bitter spirit toward the offender that will produce a deep infection in his soul that can fester for years. An old Native American proverb says, "Speak the truth; but only of the good in others." Try that. It's a really hard thing to do. But as James says, "If you can restrain your tongue, then you can restrain your whole body."

Apart from all the evil and destruction we found out that gossiping causes, the worst thing yet about its is this: when you talk wrongly about someone else, you are voluntarily closing Heaven's gates of blessing over you. You are holding back great blessings that the Lord wants to give you. With every word we say, we are sowing in the lives of others and the same sow-and-reap consequences follow, whether they be positive or negative. What do you think you will reap? When an offense is offered to you, will you be foolish enough to take it?

Early in 1997, a 26-year old man was the subject of much gossip in his church in Costa Mesa, California. He was said to be a nice young man with a friendly disposition, but the incessant gossip was too much for him. He hung himself. His suicide not merely said "Gossip kills." He was a victim of "friendly fire". Think of his parent's and friend's pain. Think of the testimony of a church and a people who kill its own! Think before you lend your tongue to the enemy!

15

The Drug Dilemma

We've heard it over and over, "Just say no to drugs", "Drugs kill", the are such a destructive habit, and they are not anything new to us anymore. We have already seen its effects all around us, but I wanted to include a small section about this powerful subject because even at that, it is something that has become so common in our day, even among professing Christians.

There was a survey taken in Harlem, New York in 1991. They found 18,000 hard drug addicts, 5,000 were children between the ages of seven to fifteen, and 90 percent of these kids lived by themselves because their parents just moved off and left them.

A fifteen year-old girl in New York who had just gotten off drugs said, "The worst mistake I ever made was experimenting with the lousy stuff." She started failing in school having horrible dreams every night, waking up in a sweat crying, screaming, she had a great memory loss, she got very lazy, didn't like herself and got slouchy with a bad attitude toward anything worthwhile.

In the last seventeen years in America, over 1 million high school kids admitted to using drugs regularly (and think of the ones who won't admit they use drugs). Every six minutes in America, a school kid's mind goes past the point of no return, because of the drugs he's taking.

Worldwide, 35 people die per day, just because of sniffing or huffing. In America alone 36 million people admitted to smoking Pot, and 20 million use it more than once a week. Pot is the number one import in America, and its total sales in the year of 1999 was 78 billion dollars. Even Nicotine, which causes throat and lung cancer, accounts for 10 billion a year, and alcohol, a drug that kills millions every year, accounts up to 48 billion a year.

In the year of 1999, the cost of drug abuse in terms of crime, clinical treatment, care and loss of work, amounted to 91 billion dollars, and heroin addicts alone accounted to 23 billion.

Today in America, it is estimated that 27 percent of our teachers, 31 percent of our lawyers, 29 percent of our judges, 31 percent of our doctors, 30 percent of our surgeons, and 24 percent of our pastors and preachers, use illegal drugs everyday. Marijuana is the widest used drug in all these categories.

Statistics also say that drug abuse is starting to get more and more common among professing Christian youth and families, can you see how they are using their influence to promote these drugs!

Statistics also say that America spends sixty times more money on alcohol, than on foreign missions, and eighteen times more money on domestic house pets, than on spreading the gospel to the un-reached. America also spends an average of 57 billion dollars on illegal drugs and 38 billion on cocaine. If these statistics were taken a few years ago, how must it be like today?

In Alaska, the Supreme Court ruled that marijuana for

The Drug Dilemma

personal use in the home was legal, but not in public. You heard me right, you can't smoke it in your car but you can in your house! Couldn't you get high at your house and then go out and drive your car? In fact, how did it get in the house in the first place?!

It's like we are giving our youth access to these drugs and then punishing them for using them! It is important to realize that 90 percent of all drug addicts started out on small things and then added other drugs to get a bigger "high" and nobody ever intended to be "hooked" and ruin their life.

The Laredo, Tx. border patrols said that during the month of July 2001, drug seizures in their sector totaled an amount of $22 million! In the fiscal year, it totaled $281 million! That's enough to create two high budget Hollywood films and feed thousands of starving children! In the year of 1999, the cost of drug abuse in terms of crime, clinical treatment, care and loss of work, amounted to 91 billion dollars, and heroin addicts alone accounted to 23 billion.

Drugs are not just a problem of today's modern culture. History records that the early Inca Indians also used drugs. A major factor in their evil practices was their addiction to the powerful drug cocaine, which they developed from the coca leaves. Their minds were so distorted that in their worship of particularly the sun god, they eventually gave him everything they had, even the lives of their children. Children at age eight or nine would be placed in the open, sun-drenched fields to die a slow, agonizing death of exposure which took several days. And even these practices of false gods had their roots in drugs because to relieve the suffering of their children, they gave them coca leaves to chew on. These leaves contained cocaine, a powerful, numbing drug to which most of the culture was addicted.

Ben Thomas, a sixteen-year-old guy from Georgia wrote the following suicidal note, "To whom it may concern: I,

Ben Thomas, am about to cause all misery caused by myself to end. I have lived a short and tragic life for me and others close to me. I have been a big disappointment to myself and my family since day one. Recently I've been in a lot of trouble (caused by drugs) causing great distress to me and my family, I have been in great depression lately and can't handle it anymore. Tell Sergeant Paterson (a narcotics officer) that I had rather be dead than a nark (a person who turns in drug dealers). I hope God has mercy on me. Goodbye, Ben Thomas."

Then he shot himself.

With all this chaos happening in our culture we still ask ourselves, "How can it be? What did we do wrong?" The answer is simple. We've turned our back from God.

Revelations 21:8 says that,"…the fearful, and unbelieving and abominable, and murderers, and whoremongers, and sorcerers, and idolaters, and all liars, shall have their part in the lake which burneth with fire and brimstone which is the second death."

The word here "sorcerers" which is literally translated "drugs" appears 27 times in the New Testament. The word "drugs" comes from the Greek word "pharimeka" which is where we get our word "pharmacy", or drug dealer.

Revelation 18:23 says, "The light of a lamp will never shine in you again. The voice of bridegroom and bride will never be heard in you again. Your merchants were the worlds great men…all the nations were led astray." In our world today there is so much deception with peoples minds being darkened and warped by drugs. Notice in the last phrase of the verse it talks about "merchants" as being the great men of the world and today wicked drug dealers sell drugs for money all over the world! Notice not only their deception but also their eternal punishment in Hell. Death, destruction, and disaster are for those who make drugs their god and do not repent and change.

Galatians 5:20 says, "The acts of the sinful nature are obvious...witchcraft..."

That word "witchcraft", is the same root word for drug abuse. So according to the Bible, witchcraft, the occult, and drug abuse go hand in hand. Add to that all the immorality in youth, many unwed mothers, and heavy metal rock music, and we have some really messed up lives.

Nevertheless, "The Lord is slow to anger, abounding in love and forgiving sin and rebellion. Yet he does not leave the guilty unpunished; he punishes the children for the sin of the fathers to the third and fourth generation." -Numbers 14:18

It is already medically and scientifically proven that if you smoke five joints of anything in your life, it will have a genetic effect, and damage body chromosomes in your seed for up to four generations! Studies also show that a person who gets high on LSD will not have all his faculties for three months. Today, because mothers abuse drugs during pregnancy, 3,200 innocent babies born every day, are victims to being hooked on drugs and began to go through drug withdrawls immediately, all because of the consequence of their parents' drug abuse. The results are obvious. Look at all the abortions and deformed babies that come every year as a result.

But in the same way, "The just man walketh in his integrity: his children are blessed after him." -Proverbs 20:7

If any kind of addiction, could make people happy, addictive people would be the happiest people in the world!

Another young guy by the name of Dexter Gardener, who was heavily involved in drugs at age seventeen said, "Life is a dead end road that has nothing to offer me. There is nothing that I haven't already tried, except Hell, so I'm going to try that." Then he also shot himself.

My dear reader, our nation is in trouble. Even the secular world knows that. She is bleeding from without, and broken and bruised from within. Her youth, the very life of the nation are being destroyed by sin and shame. I'm asking myself, could you and I have had a different answer for this young boy's life? Definitely! Because if you have Jesus in your heart, you *have* something priceless to give the world that the world desperately needs! You are desperately needed! Guy and girls lets get to work!

The following is a letter written by a young girl who had to serve a sentence in jail because of drug abuse. She received Jesus Christ as her Savior before her sentence started and I want you to see the incredible difference that this made and the attitude she had toward her circumstances.

Dear Mom,

"I am writing to ask you to ask your church to pray the week of July 5th. On that day my lawyer will file for my shock probation, so I need prayer for God's will to be done. I know, however, that I am here for a reason; that is to share my faith in Christ to the broken hearted. There is no greater joy, than to give the joy of the Lord to those who don't know Him. To see their eyes light up with new hope and life has been all worth it. I no longer feel this is a punishment for bad choices, but an opportunity to be used by my Savior to share His grace with these ladies who may never hear it anywhere but here. I will leave here with a greater understanding, of my Lord and His awesome power, than I ever thought I could. I feel the prayers of everyone for me, I have a comfort here that is beyond understanding. I am truly blessed to be walking in the presence of my Lord. It is a feeling I can't explain; as though there is an unseen blanket wrapped around my soul. I love you all and thank you for your prayers!" God bless, —Dina

What a powerful testimony! Do you see the difference in her attitude than that of the other two young men who went through the same thing. The final outcome of these peoples' lives was literally in their hands. She turned back to God, saw this as a ministry opportunity and made the most in letting God use her, even in prison, while the other two turned away from God and took their lives into their own hands and made a mess of it.

It's good to learn from your own mistakes, but it's even wiser to learn from others' mistakes and avoid a life of Hell.

As William James said, "This life is worth living, we can say, because it is what we make it."

16

Dating vs. Waiting: Which One Is God's Best?

Dating is like a princess going through the woods kissing frogs in hopes of finding a prince. She may find a prince, or she may not. Most likely she'll grow to like kissing frogs so much, she will end up marrying one.

What is the second most important decision you will make in your life, after salvation?

Definitely marriage, because it will either put you on the right path for life, or take you down the wrong path, for life. Think of it, the person you marry and spend the rest of your life with will literally make your life a success or a failure. Marriage is a big deal.

Before going on, I want to make it clear that "dating", when you're engaged and seriously planning to marry this person, is in fact, a very beautiful, natural element that God created as part of our lives. It does get to be a problem, however, when it is out from under God's perfect and unique plan that He has already designed. When I say "out from

God's plan" I mean—the "dating game" where you're of no age to marry and you just do it for fun like everyone else. This kind of "premature" dating is what we will be talking more about in the next few pages.

In a world like we live in today where relationships are superficial, commitments are shallow, marriages are shaky, divorces are nearly as common as marriage, and adultery is just another "life-style." What is wrong? If thousands of cars in America stared to break down, I can promise you that the government would be checking into it. But thousands of marriages are breaking down all over the world and no one stops to do anything about it! Isn't it about time that someone stopped and analyzed these situations and seriously said, "What is going on?!" Could it be that much of the blame for many of these problems could be laid at the feet of an unscriptural, 20th century, American phenomenon, called...DATING? I believe, and hope that if you can keep an open mind long enough to read and study this, we can find out, what is really wrong with dating?

I am very aware that many of us have played the dating game and don't see anything wrong with it. But is it Biblical? Is it God's *best* for our lives? What does the Book of Life, the guide of our youth, have to say about it? Lets see!

17

Twelve Important Things Everyone Needs To Know about "Christian" Dating

1 Thessalonians 4:3-8 says, "For this is the will of God, even your sanctification, that ye should abstain from fornication: that every one of you should know how to posses his vessel in sanctification and honor; not in the lust of concupiscence, even as the Gentiles, which know not God: that no man go beyond and defraud his brother in any matter: because that the Lord is the avenger of all such, as we also have forewarned you and testified. For God hath not called us unto uncleanness, but unto holiness. He therefore that despiseth, despiseth not man, but God, who hath also given unto us his Holy Spirit."

My paraphrased version says: "For it is God's will for you to be sanctified and set apart to holiness so that you won't get involved in immorality. If you're going to do this then you need to know how to acquire a wife in a holy way, one that shows her incredible value!

You must not tolerate lustful passions or wrong, covetous affections. That's the way the people of the world do it, who don't even know God. That no one should step over the fences God has put into place, and raise expectations that could cheat his/her "neighbor" in any way, because the Lord is the avenger of all who do these things as we have also forewarned you and given you these examples for you to read about it. Because God has called us unto holiness..."

I searched and searched for any "good explanations" for practicing "Christian dating" in the Bible and surprisingly this is what I found.

1. Christian dating robs you of the commitment of being a "one-man woman," or "one-woman-man."

My mom majored in music in college, so all of us kids grew up playing many different intruments. We have been invited many times to play for weddings and special social events like that, but there was one wedding in particular that had an great impact on my life with what we are talking about. It was held in a beautiful whitewashed church with picturesque stained glass windows and mosaic carvings on the ceiling. All the guests were seated, and the wedding was about to begin. We started to play the music to the wedding march as the beautiful bridesmaids walked down the aisle in their elegant gowns. Everyone was joyfully expectant about the event that would take place on this great day.

I saw the beautiful bride, with stars in her eyes, as she floated down the aisle on her father's arm and took her place alongside her fiancé. The whole ceremony was so wonderful, almost heavenly. Tears streamed down the faces of all the people as the bride and groom sang to each other their wedding vows. She later told me, "My husband was the first boyfriend I ever had, and he was the first guy I ever held hands with." Talk about true purity! There still *are* young people out there with a passion and purity enough to commit to be pure until the ring is on their finger.

In 2 Corinthians 11:2 God says, "For I am jealous over you with godly jealousy: for I have espoused you to *one* husband, that I may present you as a *chaste* virgin to Christ." (My italics).

How many mates does it say? One. This word here "chaste", in Greek, is *"hagnos"* meaning: blameless, innocent, clean, modest, and pure. Let's think back to this wedding I just described. Could these "witnesses" say that this bride and groom are blameless? Innocent? Clean? Pure? A chaste virgin? Could they say that they had really saved themselves just for their mate? Were they able to stand before the others without them being able to "point a finger" and say that they had done something that hadn't been reconciled?

Do you ever wonder why God didn't just make a dozen girls for Adam to have fun with before he married Eve? I don't think it would have been any problem at all for God to have made half a dozen guys and half a dozen girls, let them date around until they found the right one, and *then* marry that one. I think God could have done that! He could have made one thousand people at the same time! But He didn't. He wanted to show us something.

The perfect picture of creation is *not* that Adam is marrying Eve because God just happened to make her and there was just no one else around to check out. In the perfect wisdom of our Creator, Adam was to wait until God brought along that special, specific person that he was to marry. God wanted Adam to be a *one-woman type of a man*, and Eve to be a *one-man type of a woman*.

There was a young guy who had been studying at a Christian Bible college, and on the fourteenth of February, this college was hosting a Valentine's banquet. There was a young girl at the same college who didn't have a date, so the president of the college decided he was going to give her a date in chapel service. He found out that this young man didn't have a date to the banquet either. So then in chapel service, in front of hundreds of other students, he called out the guy's name and said, "I want you to take this girl to the Valentine's banquet." And the guy said, "But...I can't, I don't want to." Then the president of the college said, "Why not? Are you gay or something?!"

That young man left the Christian Bible college. He had felt called to go full time in the ministry, but now it is questionable if he will ever follow through or not. The blow really affected that young man. What if he just wanted to be a one-woman man? What if he just wanted to save his heart for his one true love?

In Song of Solomon 8:6, Solomon's beloved is telling him, "Set me as a seal upon thine heart, as a seal upon thine arm…" so that she would be his "one and only". Before you were ever born, God had already picked out a mate for you, and as He created you, he was also creating that special someone who, later on in life, He would bring across your path for you to marry and he/she would become your mate for life.

In the book of Exodus God has established for us certain laws, that if we will live by them, we will also reap the wonderful blessings that follow them. But if we break these laws, we will also reap the consequences that follow them. I was reading one of these verses one day and was amazed at what I read pertaining to this principle of being a one-man woman and a one-woman man.

"If a man seduces a virgin who is not pledged to be married and sleeps with her, he must pay the bride-price, and she shall be his wife. If her father absolutely refuses to give her to him, he must still pay the bride-price for virgins." — Exodus 22:16-17

In Bible days and still in some countries in other parts of the world today, they have what they call a "dowry", or bride-price, that the groom has to pay the father in order to be able to legally marry his daughter. Imagine if these Old Testament laws were still made to go into action in our world today, how many guys and girls would be left devastated by broken relationships and futureless lives? How many young, unwed mothers and teen pregnancies would there be then? Not very many.

You could say, "Well, that was the Old Testament. We are not under that law anymore."

It doesn't matter whether or not this is the Generation X, Y, or Z. The Biblical laws which God established from the beginning of time, which were recorded in the Bible are unchangeable. They work the same yesterday, today, tomorrow and forever! If God's principles of moral freedom were applied to people's live today, there would be no need for abortion clinics, divorces, family planning offices, and welfare programs. Even more than that, we have to catch the *spirit* of the law and not just the *letter* of the law. In other words, we have to trust that God had a very good reason for establishing these laws and wanting us to obey them, or He wouldn't have written so much about this in the Bible. You can be sure that God never gives us irrelevant or unnecessary warning signs.

2. Christian dating robs guys and girls, especially girls, of the sense of security in relationships.

"My world crumbled as I hung up the phone. My mind raced in confusion at the stark realization of sudden rejection and betrayal. A strange, aching pain filled my soul and body as if I had been run over by a train. I didn't want to live anymore. Staring at the blank wall, the piercing words of my girlfriend bounced around in my mind like a runaway ping pong ball. Sitting there, I knew I was awake but wished it was all a dream. She said it was over. Besides that, she was now dating my best friend. My heart broke into a thousand pieces. Two things added to the erupting pain. We were both Christians and had talked about spending the rest of our lives together. Add to that my best friend's betrayal. My heart felt insecure and strangely empty as I faced the feelings of my deep wound. For months I never felt more alone. My cries to God didn't seem to get past the ceiling."

Sounds familiar? This isn't anything new. Every girl's dream is to get married, and every girl's nightmare is to break up. Hearts are ripped apart by broken relationships every day. Pop tunes echo our failed quest for true love again and again. Country music bellows out the agony we experience when we can't find true love. Soul music stirs us to relieve the pain of loneliness when "our baby" leaves us. On and on it goes. Movies and soap operas depict our fantasy search for that "one love" that will fulfill our every need. We crave for the soul mates of our dreams.

But can this security be found in another human being? We could tell story after sad story about our search for love and security in all the wrong places. But true security can't be found in horizontal relationships, but vertical. It can't be found in another human being, but in God alone. You are only as secure as that to which you have secured yourself. True security comes from living a life that is built around what is eternal, lasts forever, and cannot be destroyed, damaged, or taken away by the things of this world. Idolatry is expecting from other people or things what only God can give you, and definitely, security is something that only God can give you.

There was a young girl at a Christian college who recently resigned her position as secretary of their missions prayer band. She had been dating the guy who was voted this year's president of the prayer band. They had broken up, but he wouldn't leave her alone and she couldn't take it any longer. So this beautiful, young girl, who had such a strong passion for Jesus, and a genuine burden for missions, surrendered her position of usefulness in the ministry, due to this whole mess.

Do you realize how much the Lord could use you as soon as you develop a sincere relationship, in total security, with Him? God has already designed human life in such a way that if guys would be strong young men of God and follow the principles of His word, then we, as girls can feel secure from the cradle to the grave! If we are called to be different from the world, then the way you get a mate is not supposed to be like the world either!

Un-consciously what you do and the seeds you sow *before* marriage will produce fruit *after* marriage. It gets to be a whole time consuming lifestyle because we will do things like shop around for clothes according to what we think our crush likes, and everywhere we go, whether to the church, mall, school, store, supermarket, library or just around the block, we are "on the prowl" and on the lookout! It's crazy!

(We're supposed to be trying to please God not guys!) The worst part of it all is that when it comes time for marriage, these guys and girls will later be looking for the cutest guy or girl around. But think of this for just a minute…what good is all this going to be *after* marriage? What good will this be in fifty years? By then, will he/she look as cute and glamorous as fifty years ago? Remember…*all that glitters isn't gold!* Could this be one main reason why many couples divorce and then re-marry some "beauty queen," just to go through all this again?

It was February 14th, we were celebrating my Dad's birthday, and Mom had bought him a delicious heart-shaped strawberry cake. You know, dating is like a cake. The more pieces of your heart, you give out, the fewer you will have left for your future mate, and when that day comes (and believe me it will!) when you stand at the altar to give your *whole* heart away. Will it really be the "whole" or just another piece? I remember a popular, secular song called, "The Shape of my Heart". What would be the shape of one's heart after there are so many missing pieces because of playing the dating game?

Going back to the original title, instead of clinging to your boyfriend/girlfriend for security and fulfillment, these normal feelings are to re-direct us back to God, as we pour our heart and our feelings out to Him in prayer. If your passions are aroused, say so-to yourself and to God, *not* to the object of your passion!

3. Christian dating violates the command to "not go beyond and defraud."

The word "defraud" comes from the Latin root *de* which means "down" and *fraudo* which means "to cheat". So, to defraud is to cheat, to covet, to overreach, overstep, get an advantage, make a gain, or withhold from another what you caused him or her to expect from you. One way to defraud is emotionally. You can emotionally defraud, playing the dating game, without playing it any other way at all. That's why Proverbs 4:23 says, "Guard your heart with all diligence; for out of it are the issues of life." It takes diligence to guard your heart. It isn't just a thing of one time, but every single time something comes up. So guard your heart *and* emotions, and don't trade it in for pleasure.

What happens with Christian dating is that we are putting up a fence to "protect" the *physical* endangerment, and not the *emotional* endangerment. But that's not God's way! Because with this fence up, it still creates a desire that

"Christian" Dating

can only be righteously fulfilled after marriage. God's way puts the fence up for the emotional endangerment as well. *Human emotions are not children's toys to be played with!*
    In dating, a common question is, "How far is too far?"
    Imagine a girl and a guy get into a car and they go for a ride. Pretty soon they come to the top of a hill and they start rolling down it at top speed. There just flying downhill and having a great time...until they see they're headed for a giant brick wall! Suddenly, they look around and realize that there are no brakes! Who would make a car with no brakes? Not General Motors! God does. Because no brakes are needed when it's God's way. Not knowing what to do, they soon slam into the brick wall and end in disaster. Going "through the wall" is when disaster hits, but when did this all start? When they both started at the top of the hill. Did they think they would hit the wall when they started? No! You know you have gone too far *after* you've gone too far. So don't get into the car to begin with! Sexual immorality can be forgiven, but it causes pain like no other sin can.
    I once heard a pastor share this story about a fairly large church that was heavily involved in Christian dating: "I had been giving a series of teachings that week to this church when a family from there came up to talk to me. They said, "Everything at our church and school is built around dating and we don't know what to do." Seriously, my first thought was, "It's probably not as bad as it seems, I know the church's pastor, he's a wise man of God and he's probably built enough Biblical principles around it to protect them even if they don't realize it." So I asked them, "Just how bad is it?" He answered, "Five young girls of our Christian school graduated pregnant this year, and it happens the same every year."
    You see, God put up two boundaries, the emotional and the physical, and when you cross one, you'll be more tempted to cross the other one too. If you don't properly protect the

soul, then you can't properly protect the body either. People now days are trying to deal with the problems of physical relationships in young people without dealing with all the other root problems that relate to it. The *real* problem is, that in our little Christian world of today, we are trying to take something of the world, clean it up a little, add the word

"Christian", and then say its fine! We're trying to get "substitutes" for the things of the world. *It hasn't worked, it isn't working and it won't work!*

There was a guy and a girl who had been going out for quite a while, until one day the girl decided it was over and she broke up with him. He tried to get her back, but she wasn't interested. So he drove over to her house, parked in her driveway, beeped the horn until she came to the door, and then he put a gun to his head and shot himself to death.

He was foolishly willing to pay any price to get back any of the emotional ties he had lost.

Another family gave this testimony. "When our daughter was younger, we had never heard of any other way than dating. My husband and I thought we were protecting her enough by the rules we made regarding the guy she dated. She was protected from the physical dangers that we as parents felt. Over the years we realized she was not protected from the emotional trauma of dating. When her latest dearly beloved decided he didn't love her anymore, she became despondent, and unable to keep anything on her stomach. I knew she was sad and tried to comfort her, but was unaware that she wasn't eating well until I received a call from her workplace saying that they had taken her to the hospital. She had collapsed from dehydration. Eventually she recovered physically, but what about emotionally? When she finds her husband-to-be, will she be able to truly trust him with her heart? Will there be doubt because of betrayed trust in the past? Can the *hormone high* of dating be more important than the safety, contentment, and peace of mind that comes from waiting for the Lord's perfect timing? My daughter's experience may be extreme but trust me, you won't miss a thing by waiting, except depressing, emotional baggage."

Proverbs 5:15-20 says, "Drink waters out of *thine own* cistern, and running waters out of *thine own* well. Let thy fountains be dispersed abroad, and rivers of waters in the streets.

Let them be *thine own*, and not strangers' with thee. Let thy fountains be blessed and rejoice with the wife of thy youth...And why wilt thou, my son, be ravished with a strange woman, and embrace the bosom of a stranger?" (My italics)

When God talked to the children of Israel about this issue, He had already given them many chances and He said, "How shall I pardon thee for this?...when I had fed them to the full, they then committed adultery...they were as fed horses in the morning: every one neighed after his neighbor's wife" —Jeremiah 5:7-8

The greatest mistake about dating is that when you play the dating game, you are actually messing around with your "neighbor's" husband or wife. She or he is not really yours! She/he already belongs to someone, because God, in his perfect plan, has already included and reserved a mate for you. That's how perfect and precise God's plan for each one of our lives is!

4. Christian dating robs you of your purity

If you're like me, I think most of us look at purity like a line, or a boundary that we shouldn't cross. But actually it is much different than a line. With a line, you can get as close or as far away from it as you want, *before* you actually cross it. True purity, as Jesus wants for us, is more like thermometer that measures up to how much purity you have, how much you have already given away, and how much you can regain.

Girls: Romans 14:13 says, "that no man put a stumbling block or an occasion to fall, in his brother's way." God created girls and guys to think differently. While we are on the emotional side with relationships, guys battle with their eyes and keeping their thoughts pure. We can help them so much if we would take note of this and try to protect them, avoiding actions and appearance that could cause them to stumble and fall. As one young guy put it, "A girl can't simply dress according to what *she* feels is right, because what she feels is right for her, might not be right for a guy to look at."

I have to say that if you're a girl and you're reading this, you might think, *"Well, maybe the guy needs to get his life right. Maybe he needs to guard his thoughts better."* All I'm trying to say, girls, is that you have the power to help guys, by dressing and acting modestly. I know you might not want to hear what I'm about to say, but if you have a question about what you're wearing, talk to your Dad. Say, "Hey, Dad, what do you think about this?" Dads have a good idea what's right most of the time.

Guys: What does the Bible mean when it talks about us girls as the "weaker vessel?" It means this: that we can be emotionally damaged more easily than a man, so our emotions must be protected. If you asked the majority of girls, we would tell you we would much rather prefer to be in the company of a guy that we know will protect us anytime, anywhere, than in the company of someone who will be like a "hunter on the lookout" or a "tiger on the prowl" ready to pounce!

Mathew 26:41 says, "Watch and pray, that ye enter not into temptation: the spirit indeed is willing, but the flesh is weak." Your flesh is weak! You could say, "But I read the Bible and go to church, and pray every day and fast!" That's great! Wonderful! I hope you do go to church and read the

"Christian" Dating

Bible and pray and fast, I hope you do great things for God! But...your flesh is still weak. You can never grow *enough* spiritually to the place where you can trust the flesh. We can see this over and over in the lives of ministers and great Christian men of God who fall into this type of sin. They get to the point of believing the lie of Satan that, "that could never happen to me", and that's when they fall (or should I say "dive" into immorality). A.N. Martin said, "You can only get into the realm of deliberate sin when you get out of the realm of the fear of God." John Dryden said, "Better shun the bait than struggle in the trap." Sin blinds, binds, and then grinds.

A young guy was upset because his father wouldn't let him go out alone, in a car with a girl. He said, "But what's wrong Dad, don't you trust me?" His father replied, "In a car? Alone? At night? With a girl? I wouldn't trust myself son, why should I trust you?!"

And you think this is just a problem among teens?! I've seen plenty of "goo-goo eyed" 30, 40 and 50 year-olds still running around with "boyfriends" and "girlfriends!"

Another girl's parents were leaders in their church. When she turned thirteen, the parental role went right into place. No dating before sixteen. Then in the spring of ninth grade, at the age of fourteen, she begged her Mom and Dad to let her go out with a guy who had just turned sixteen, had just gotten his drivers license, and was going to be moving away. An hour and a half of time away from the house seemed logical and safe, surely there wouldn't be any problem with that. The boy's family were regular members of the same +church, he was regularly involved with youth activities, what could possibly go wrong?

It was an hour and a half that had not ended years later. Those teens got sexually involved in that time away from their parents, and probably no one will ever know all that happened, but everything changed. The girl was shattered, humiliated and confused. She got home and blurted out everything to her mother. The boy, confronted by his own mother after a phone call from this girls' parents, admitted what had happened and then exploded with these words, "Momma, that girl is nothing but a slut and a whore!" Thus two young lives were irreparably damaged for the rest of their earthly stay. Those hurts would have not had to be if someone had realized that...*dating is a threat to purity!*

In a previous eight-year period, 100 million dollars were spent in the state of Illinois, in order to combat teenage pregnancies. Then they did a little research and found out that they couldn't tell it had done any good at all. Why hadn't it? Because they had not checked into the root cause!

Statistics also say that one out of four university girls are involved in "date" rape. Now do you think that would happen if teens talked together and associated in group activities? Would it happen if family and friends were present?

You can spend all the money you want to trying to combat the problem of teenage pregnancies, but as long as you continue in the society, as our society is presently doing saying, "Dating is fine! We have no problem with our guys and girls spending time together alone, we trust them!" Then you're going to continue to have teenage unwed mothers. That doesn't matter whether it is in the world or the church, the results are going to continue with the same consequences coming upon us.

Think about the examples that are given to us in the Bible: Solomon, the wisest man on earth, Samson, the strongest man who ever lived, and David, a man after God's own heart. Now if you can't trust the flesh of a judge of Israel like Samson, or a man after God's own heart like David, how can you trust the flesh of a teenager?

It is also true that some people are still "technically" virgins, but that's all. Just one night of your life spent wrong will change your future forever, and result in a lifetime of consequences. It scares me to think of how many more sweet, dedicated, Christian young guys and girls are going to have to loose their virtue and purity, before pastors, parents, and churches wake up to realize that...*dating is a threat to purity!*

"Can a man take fire in his bosom, and his clothes not be burned? Can one go upon hot coals, and his feet not be burned? So he that goeth in to his neighbors wife; whosoever toucheth her shall not be innocent." —Proverbs 6:27-29 KJV

Sin may be fun for the moment, but it carries an extremely high price tag.

5. Christian dating violates the Biblical command that Christians are supposed to treat each other like brothers and sisters.

What is it about the brother-sister relationship that is right for guys and girls until they're really headed for the marriage alter?

Brothers and sisters aren't always chasing after each other trying to date each other! They have the freedom to get to know each other just the way they are. Any brother can carry a package, or open the door for any sister at anytime. Any brother can pick up anything for any sister and be nice to her at anytime.

Think of a guy and girl on a date, the way they treat each other when they're going out is totally different than when they weren't. After they break up, you tell me if they go back to treating each other as brothers and sisters! Brother-sister relationships don't have to change, they don't deceive each other and don't have to suffer broken relationships because theirs never has to break.

I remember the friendly, but good response of a friend

toward a guy wanting to date her, she said, "What do you want, that you think you will get out of a "dating" relationship, that a regular friendship does not give?" That really got him thinking twice! However, never give yourself the excuse "He's like a brother" to get away with wrong actions or attitudes.

One time I "interviewed" a couple from our church who were going out. I asked one them story of how they had gotten together. They told me that, typically, it happened at a youth camp. He had a crush on her, and she was just as crazy for him, (really just because he was one of the few guys who had crushes on her). They started sending each other little notes during church, calling each other on the phone, he even started coming to her house with the excuse of giving her "free guitar lessons", so they could be together more often. All the guys were pressuring him to ask her out, and she along with all the other girls were passing word around with every little word, phone call, and "love letter", about every detail and move he made. Soon, nineteen-year-old Alex and eighteen-year-old Sarah started going out with the ultimate "goal" of marriage; but until then, the mindset of "let's see what happens". I watched this relationship develop for over two years, and if you watched them, they seemed to absolutely adore each other—already speaking of wedding plans, and a future family. They seemed to be "inseparable."

After over three years of their relationship, however, suddenly and abruptly, and for no logical reason at all, Sarah decided she had had enough of it because she wanted to hurry up and get married and Alex didn't feel he was quite ready yet for marriage, so they broke up. After all that had happened over the years, you can imagine how big a devastation this was not only for Alex and Sarah, but for both their families, their friends, their pastor, and all the other members of their church. It was so hard because before when something like this had happened, one of the families left

"Christian" Dating

the church, so everyone was thinking in their minds, "I wonder who will be the one to leave this time." We dreaded it to happen because both were actively involved in church activities such as participating in the music on Sunday mornings and helping out in meetings all throughout the week.

Going back to the beginning of this story, where did this all start? At a youth camp where they were both supposed to be wholeheartedly seeking after a closer and deeper walk with God! Do you think dating would be even a little bit Biblical, when eventually, its whole main focus and goal is to "get to know each other better" and "see what happens" rather than grow closer to God?

I asked Sarah what her parents thought about this from the very beginning, and she said they told her, "Just don't break his heart." Someone asked them if they had even stopped to ask God what *He* thought about it. They weren't very sure, but according to Alex and Sarah, they said they both "prayed" about this all before it happened. So I ask myself, "What could have gone wrong?" I think I found the answer with this second couple I "interviewed".

Kyle and Kristen were introduced at a Rotary club waffle supper by Kristen's brother-in- law. Kyle was 24, and Kristen had just turned 17. Several years prior to that, Kristen had made a commitment to the Lord not to date but to wait on God for Him to bring her a Godly husband in His perfect timetable. At the waffle supper, Kyle sat with Kristen's family, and there discovered that he attended their church! Over the next two years, Kristen and her family became close friends with Kyle and his family. He truly became like a son to the Flournoys' and like a brother to Kristen. As Kristen and Kyle became better acquainted, the Lord began to reveal to them the character qualities in one another that each had been desiring in a marriage partner. However, Kyle thought she would think he was too old and would not be interested. Kristen thought he felt she was too young and would not be interested. Both guarded their emotions fiercely and never gave any indication of a potential romantic interest. The following year, Kristen began noticing a difference in Kyle. He seemed more attentive to her, though in no way could he be considered flirtatious. Without knowing each others thoughts, they both began privately praying that God's will would unfold.

Eighteen months prior to that, Kyle's parents had visited him and met Kristen. They had begun to ask him, "What about that Flournoy girl?" when he would be discouraged about finding a Godly wife. Also a close friend (whose child Kristen had babysat) told Kyle that Kristen possessed the great qualities to be a great wife, and he told his whole Sunday school class to pray for God to bring Kyle a Godly wife! Then on Sunday, April 2, Kyle, having received the Lord's blessing, asked Kristen's parents permission to court her, with the intention of marrying her. Permission was granted, and nineteen days later, Kyle proposed marriage in a beautiful setting on his family ranch.

Kyle and Kristen made a commitment to one another the day they began courting to wait until their wedding day to share their first kiss. What a wedding night! Since then, the Lord, in precious ways, has developed a pure, sweet, tender love between them, and they believe He has more chapters to write in their love story!

What was the difference between the two couples?

While Alex and Sarah were not single-mindedly seeking to serve God and trust him to bring along their life's mate. Kyle and Kristen were wholeheartedly trusting God to bring His choice of a life's mate, in His perfect time, and by His perfect process. Where they were always seeking the best for the other person, without any hidden personal rewards as their motives; unconsciously, Alex and Sarah had secret, selfish motives toward each other of "what can I get out of this", not "what can I give", which is the main damaging element in dating. It causes both parties to "focus on each other" instead of on God. Alex and Sarah didn't wait for anything, Kyle and Kristen sought the full approval of parents, waited, prayed and sought God about the matter even before getting involved in anyway. They were both wholeheartedly pursuing after God and spending their teen years serving Him without being concerned about finding a spouse, and when the time came, God made it clear to them. This story has become a powerful testimony for all the generations to come after them.

Time after time it has been proven that when something does not have a rock-solid foundation to be built upon from the very start, it will grow shaky and wobbly and, with the test of time, it will never stand. When we play the dating game and going through all this emotional trauma and break-ups, how is it possible for us to show God's love to our unsaved friends, which are our neighbors?! Both things totally contrast each other! They are opposites! Just as plain as night and day, or hot and cold. Reality is that perfect love, like 1 Corinthians 13 describes, is far from the "dating" love in its cause and effect.

6. Even Christian dating involves deceitfulness

Bethany was riding in the bus one afternoon on a missions trip with a team of Christian youth from her church. They were returning from evangelizing in a poor neighboring village. On that same team was a guy named Jeremy who had a crush on Bethany. During the bus ride, Jeremy was asking the other guys of his dorm what he should do and how he should act to get her attention (even though she could care less!). Bethany was in the seat right behind the guys so she heard their whole conversation (and I think they knew it too). This is a little of their conversation.

Jeremy said to John, "Am I doing the right thing? You have got to help me out! I really don't know how to get any girls' attention." John said, "No problem. You're talking to an expert in that area! Trust me, I'll give you all the tips you need. Oh, one thing that is very important. Don't get that stumped look on your face when she talks to you, and don't smile so much, just kind of twitch your eyebrows up, like this." John said, giving him a slight "demonstration." "And about your clothes...these shirts," he said with a frown, fingering his collar. "They're not very stylish, you know. Go to Old Navy. Get yourself some Silver Tabs, or Tommy Hilfigers', (the popular "in" thing at the time) cool stuff like that."

Everyone in the whole bus was rolling with laughter because Jeremy, obviously foolish was like, "Hey, anyone got a pen and a paper, this is good stuff! I got to write all these things down!" We couldn't believe it! In Bethany's mind she was thinking, "I would rather put up with a guy acting as ignorant as he *really* is, any day, than one to put on a really cool front of what he is not."

After flirting, you tend to put on a front trying to impress your date and get them to like you. Have you done that? Have you ever seen a girl with such a rotten attitude, who all at once becomes incredibly sweet?! Or a guy who is normally so disrespectful to his mother that it is absurd, then all at once he is so kind, nice, gentle, sweet, and respectful to his girl!

Girls: How many of you act the same way around your date as you act around your Dad? Guys: How many of you act the same way around your date as you act around your Mom?

Imagine, here is Matthew coming over to Suzy's house to pick her up for a date.

Matthew doesn't hear the conversation, but just before he gets there, Suzy and her Dad are having it out. Dad says,

"Christian" Dating

"Suzy you *are* going to be home by ten thirty!" Suzy sasses back, "Dad, nobody but nerds get home by ten thirty! You are just being ridiculous and unfair as usual!"

Then, there comes a knock on the door...and with sugar and spice and everything nice, Suzy croons, "Oh, Matthew darling, I'm so glad you're here! Wait just one minute, Daddy and I were just having a little conversation."

Who is the real girl? Would the real Suzy please stand up? The real Suzy was the one sassing her Dad, and if Matthew marries her, he'll find that out later. Since both of these young people are putting up a front, they'll both end up with someone different than they thought they were getting. How many times have you heard this statement from divorced couples, "Well, he's just not the same person I married!" As Dr. S.M. Davis put it,

"Everyone is looking for an ideal, but instead they marry a raw deal, now their marriage is an ordeal, and they're looking for a new deal."

7. Christian dating robs you of your emotional stability.

Dating, by its own nature, promotes feeling of rejection and low self-esteem. Common sense can tell you that!

Girls: What happens when everyone has a boyfriend, except you? What happens when you discover your crush is going out with another girl? Talk about real inner pain!

Guys: What happens when everyone has a date, except you? Then what happens when a girl turns you down when you ask her? How do you feel? When even mature adults have trouble dealing with rejection, how much more for us as teens since our emotions are not yet totally mature?

The following is a true story about a young girl who went to a psychiatrist for help.

"In February I met this guy and we got along really well.

He asked me to go out with him, and I agreed. and after only three weeks of us having met, we were boyfriend and girlfriend. Everything was going fine, he comes from a good family with good family traditions, and more than once he told me that I was his dream come true. To tell you the truth, in the beginning, I wasn't as excited as he was, and on some occasions I preferred to go out with my friends or do something else other than spend my time with him. When we first started going out, he asked me if we could see each other everyday, to get to know each other better, and everyone in my family just loved him, and everyone got along well. Very often he brought me flowers, wrote me letters, and different things like that, and after about three months, I deeply fell in love with him. I started changing in many ways and being more affectionate toward him, even though I tend to have an explosive temperament, and I get upset and irritated very easily.

After we had been going out for about five months, I started feeling how distant he was becoming from me, he didn't come to visit so often, he didn't bring me flowers anymore, and didn't tell me he loved me anymore. I asked him what had happened and he told me he didn't know. He wanted to go to work in America, so I told him that then we would probably have to break up, and it might be better that we stopped seeing each other so often. I got out of the car and went inside my house, thinking that this was just another discussion between us and that the next day everything would go back to being normal again. Many days went by, I went to look for him, I cried and told him I still loved him, I begged him to come back and told him that he was still so very dear to my heart, and that I wanted to be with him forever. He said no and told me that he didn't want to be with me any longer and that I shouldn't make matters worse. I asked him to look at me in the eyes and if it was really true, and say that he didn't love me anymore. And

"Christian" Dating

with tears in his eyes he said, "I don't love you anymore, and I don't want to be with you any longer." That night was the worst night in my whole life. I am very heartbroken and I don't know what to do, I think I've lost him forever. I would be forever grateful to you if you could recommend some kind of therapy, or some book, just anything to heal this deep pain I have in my heart."

The newspaper told another story about a twelve year-old girl who had a crush on a guy, but he liked another girl. And because of her feelings of rejection, this girl accused this guy and his best friend of raping her. Both him and his friend were arrested and put in jail. One of them faced charges that would keep him in jail until thirty years of age, and the other friend until the age of twenty-one. Finally, after the girl realized what a mess she'd gotten herself into, she admitted it was all false. She was then arrested and put into a juvenile detention center, her parents were told, "Either you find a permanent place for her, or we will."

Another seventeen year-old boy was at a public high school with his girlfriend, but after dating for a while, she broke up with him and walked away with another guy. That seventeen year-old boy, stung by feelings of rejection, went home, pulled out a shotgun and killed himself.

In May of 1992, a fourteen year-old boy, who studied at a high school in Oklahoma City, OK., unexpectedly pulled out a shotgun and shot another seventeen year-old classmate in the head. It was over…a girl. He later said, "If I hadn't shot him, then he might have shot me, besides that's the way they do it on TV."

In February of 1994 a news broadcast said that Atlanta police were looking for a twelve year-old girl accused of shooting another thirteen year-old girl. And it was over…a boy.

In St. Louis, Mo., an eighteen year-old high school girl was sentenced to life in prison for the shooting death of her ex-boyfriend in a school hallway. This happened after he had dumped her about two weeks before the shooting.

Sometimes we do hear about the fist fights and word fights that go on in schools among guys over the girls, but we don't hear about all the school shootings that are for this same reason. Statistics live to tell the tale but the saddest part of it is these horror stories will continue until someone realizes that *dating is a threat to emotional stability!*

8. Christian dating violates the principle of "going to sleep" and waiting on God to wake you up.

That's what God did for Adam in Genesis 2:21, "And the Lord God caused a deep sleep to fall upon Adam, and he slept..."

Both the picture and the principle are a perfect description of the perfect way to find a mate. Here Adam is looking around and God tells him, "Go to sleep! Forget it and just go to sleep!" And in a little while He made Eve, she was just right. God had just *one* for Adam and she was perfect. Then He woke him up and said, "Adam, look over there!" and Adam said, "Wow! She's just what I was wanting!" So what is the message? Forget about it, go to sleep, concentrate on serving God, realize the great opportunity, potential, and testimony you can have as a young person dedicated to serving God. Your potential is astounding!

The dating spirit is like a "small giant" in our lives. Small because many times we don't realize it is really there, and it's a giant because it is a huge factor that makes up our lives as young people and we don't realize its destruction until after the damage has been done.

You can't imagine how much it can distract you and cause you to miss out on that special calling that God has for your life.

"Christian" Dating

1 Corinthians 7:32-34 clearly states this issue, "But I would have you without carefulness. He that is unmarried careth for the things that belong to the Lord, how he may please the Lord: but he that is married careth for the things that are of the world, and how he may please his wife. There is difference also between a wife and virgin. The unmarried woman careth for the things of the Lord, that she may be holy both in body and in spirit: but she that is married careth for the things of the world, how she may please her husband. And this I speak for your own profit...that ye may attend upon the Lord without distraction."

Notice in the first verse, it's talking to the guys there and it never says, "He that is unmarried careth for the things of his girlfriend and how he may please her." And in the next paragraph it's talking to the girls and it doesn't say, "The unmarried woman careth for the things of her boyfriend, and how she may please him." And this verse ends saying (in my paraphrased version) "And I am telling you this for your own good...so you can get busy serving the Lord without any distractions." God knows how distracted you get when you're around you-know-who, that's why He included this in the Bible!

Stay asleep until God whacks you over the head, (He may have to whack you twice if you're good and asleep!) and says, "Look at that girl over there! She's the one!" And you can be sure He will wake you up, He is God! Or God may point out someone to your parents or your pastor, then they can all talk to her folks. Don't be constantly on the prowl! People's justification is, "But I've got to get married!" When Adam started worrying about where his helpmeet was, God said, "Don't worry about it, go to sleep and I'll wake you up *when it's time!*"

In Song of Solomon, the lover's book of the Bible, there is a scripture that is repeated three times (2:7, 3:5, and 8:4), so I think it's really important! It says, "Daughters of

Jerusalem, I charge you by the gazelles and by the does of the field, *do not arouse or awaken love until it so desires.*" (My italics).

It seems like more and more today people are plagued with feeling of loneliness and think marriage will make them happy. In one newspaper's add for singles, a divorced lady wrote, "Looking for a prince, kissed enough frogs." Yeah I bet! Another divorced man wrote this after describing his perfect girl, "When I love I love forever." Sure!

Sometimes youth tell me, "But I'm tired of being single!"

Before you're married Satan will lie to you and say, "What?! You're not married?! All of your friends are but you're not? You're totally missing out on life!" Then after you're married he'll whisper in your ear, "Look at all those dirty diapers and runny noses...think before you were married...you didn't have any of that. You were totally free!"

Don't listen! Finding *contentment* in every stage of your life is the key. You will never be truly happy in this area until you come to the point of realizing that a husband or wife can never make you truly happy. To find true contentment, instead of adding to your desires, subtract from your wants. Wake up to see the beauty of singleness! Don't do something *about* your teen years, do something *with* your teen years, because someday you will have to stand before God and give account on how you spent it. Make the most of your single years! Conquer the world while you're at it!

If it's a baby's first tooth, first haircut, first birthday, first day of school, etc., "firsts" are always a big thing to remember. I remember the day after I started learning to play the guitar, my Dad went out and bought me my first guitar pick, and I thought that was the greatest thing in the world!

With dating, if a guy and a girl would do all that is in their power to save their first love for each other, it would create an incredibly powerful bond between them, after they get married. Remember you only have one first. If you've already given away your first love, don't keep playing the dating game and shredding your heart to more pieces!

9. Christian dating stunts spiritual growth.

The dating game has become like a "god" in our culture, even among many Christians. How many Christian youth do you know, spend the same amount of time reading and studying the Bible, as they do spending time with their girlfriend/boyfriend? And how many times have you seen this happen? A girl won't go on a missions trip with her youth group in the summer, because her boyfriend won't be able to go. A guy can't go to serve someplace where there is a need because he will be away from his girlfriend for too long. A girl will not totally commit herself to serve God in her church because she is afraid of what her boyfriend will do or say when he hears about it. A guy won't totally give himself to serve the Lord and grow in a closer walk with Him because he 'won't look so cool' for his girlfriend and he is afraid that he will loose her if he doesn't.

How many times have you seen this happen? A guy (or girl) will have been going faithfully to a wonderful church and this has been his church since he was a little kid! Then suddenly he "disappears" and you never see him there again. Everyone is wondering where he went and comes to find out, he's gone to another church, or he's backslid. My first question is, "Was it over a girl?" And the answer is usually the same.

Eric was a young man of twenty-five and on the board of leaders in the church. At this age he thought to himself that it was about time for him to begin seeking his mate. There was another young girl in this same church, that he liked, her name was Susan. She was very beautiful and really had a heart for God, she sang with the praise and worship team and she was around the same age as Eric, so soon they were "going out".

This went on for a few months and they both seemed like a perfectly happy couple. But then one day suddenly Eric thought to himself and "felt" it probably wasn't really God's will for Susan to be his mate for life. So he broke up with her. Susan, however, feeling emotionally deceived, disillusioned, and betrayed, suffered just another traumatizing heartbreak. In fact she and her whole family were so upset about this whole ordeal, and she could not even bear to see Eric again, and they decided to leave the church. A few months later Susan started going out with another guy from her new church, who became her future husband and again Eric started going out with another beautiful Christian girl, from his church, named Laura.

Laura was the pastor's daughter, although she was only nineteen, petite and beautiful, she also really loved the Lord, and this time Eric just knew she was the one to be his wife. So here it started all over again, and they started going out. I remember I would watch them and think, "Oh, what a perfect couple, he's a good looking guy, she's beautiful, they both love God and desire to serve him in the ministry, and they seem so perfect for each other, in every aspect."

Then as the months went by, again, for some reason Eric decided that Laura was not really "The One" either, so they broke up. Laura, deeply hurt by feelings of rejection went through a tougher time than anyone will ever know and she thought that no one would ever want to marry her again. It took her quite a while to get over it and when she did, she decided she would have no more to do with dating around, and she waited for God to be the one to bring around the right one. Years later, God did bring around the right one and they got married.

Do you think Laura's searching and dating around with

"Christian" Dating

others, resulted in her finding this "right one", years later? Not at all. In fact she would have walked to the marriage altar a happier bride, free from guilt and heartache and pain, if she would just have been patient and waited on God, and none of this past would have ever taken place.

There is no better time in a person's life when spiritual growth is as important, as the time of youth. In fact, this is the time when you should be the closest to God because you are about to make the second greatest decision in your life!

"Remember now thy Creator in the days of thy youth, while the evil days come not, nor the years draw nigh..." - Ecclesiastes 12:1

That word "youth" in the original text means "one's present state of existence," so here is really relates to everyone at whatever age they are now.

Once you get involved in the dating game, everything else seems to take a back seat, the boyfriend/girlfriend game becomes an all consuming passion, and it even get to be like a constant battle in your mind, "He loves me, he loves me not", "She loves me, she loves me not". And these days, age doesn't even matter anymore. Younger siblings look up to their older brothers as role models. The younger generation is looking up to this generation to copy it's ways, except sadly the next generation that comes can be worse than the one before, because of a lack of a true, Godly example demonstrated in *our* lives.

Eighteen year-old Ashley, whom I met at a youth camp had started coming to church and had just gotten saved. I really liked Ashley a lot because she so inspired in me a true hunger for Christ because she was so committed to God and His calling on her life. She never missed a single meeting at church and participated in all the youth events. Then a few years later, she got involved in the "deadly" dating game. From then on, she turned her back on God, started living with her boyfriend, and soon became pregnant. All the potential I saw in her, all the great things God could have done with her life, just crumbled to the ground. I knew that God was just waiting for her to take the next step in her Christian walk with Him so He could unfold all His exciting plans for her life! But she gave the enemy that tiny piece of ground in her life through dating, and he took advantage of it all and destroyed her whole life. Satan would love to break your heart (through dating) and then contaminate it! It's the same method he uses over and over!

I'm sure you have seen these kind of a things happen before, in your life or in the lives of your friends, because *dating is a threat to spiritual growth.* Just as one man cannot serve two masters, a guy and a girl that are dating each other will find it very difficult to concentrate on serving God and instead concentrate on each other. They will lean more toward one or the other.

Dating will rob you of your opportunity to serve others and make an impact in this world now that you are young, which is when you have even more potential! This world so desperately needs youth that are truly committed to the Lord Jesus Christ and are willing to give their lives for the cause of Christ, without any earthly, temporary distractions! It has been proven and I can promise you that when you're dating or in a romantic relationship with someone, you can never think or act rationally or logically! Much less focus on God!

10. Christian dating robs you of being ready to marry when you begin seeking your bride.

"Prepare thy work without, and make it fit for thyself in the field; and afterwards build thine house." —Proverbs 24:27 KJV

Dating is built on entertainment. What do you normally do on a date? Dinner and a movie. Entertainment! But is that

"Christian" Dating

all of marriage? No! You say, "Well how can I practice and get experience to be a good wife/husband in marriage?" A great pianist who plays Chopin didn't start out playing these hard compositions. He began by practicing shorter easier pieces. What am I trying to say by this? If you will become skilled at loving and serving your family and communicating with your parents, then you can slide right into marriage with no trouble at all. So don't sit around dreaming, prepare yourself for life! Focus on *becoming* the right person instead of *searching* for the right person.

Girls ask yourself, *"Am I the kind of girl my kind of guy would want to marry?"* Guys ask yourself, *"Am I the kind of guy my kind of girl would want to marry?"*

In marriage people say, "It's 50/50." No it's not, it's 100/0! True love is all about sacrificial giving. Not my will by Thy will be done. The best preparation for marriage is to learn to die to self. Do more than your part!

A person that rides on a horse who isn't mature yet, will be taken a certain distance for a while, then whenever the horse decides, he will dump his rider. The horse has all a mind of his own, and when he isn't ready and mature enough for his will to be submitted to his riders' will, one or both could be seriously hurt and they won't arrive safely to their destination.

The same principle works for a young guy and girl before they get married. God may have created them for each other, and it may be His perfect will for them to get married, but if they don't wait patiently, and pray for God's perfect timing, then it will be difficult for them to get to their destination, the marriage alter, safely.

When God woke Adam up, it was time for him to get married. In Genesis 24, when Abraham sought a wife for his son, Isaac and Rebekah were both ready to get married. We also have to realize that our flesh is going to be trying to wake us up too. We have to be able to discern the difference between the two. The flesh and the Spirit. A good tip to remember is if you are not ready physically, spiritually, financially, mentally, and emotionally, to get married, then it wasn't God who woke you up. Go back to sleep!

One 13 year-old boy sent his girlfriend her first flowers with this note: "With all my love and most of my allowance." Was he ready to get married?

There was another story about a 12 year-old boy who went up to a 10 year-old girl and said, "Do you want to be my girlfriend?" She said, "Oh yes! What do I do?" This "love" only lasted one week!

At a Christian church camp, there was a guy there around sixteen or seventeen, and young girl came up to him and asked him, "Do you have a girlfriend yet?" He said, "No, I don't." She said, "Well, I got one picked out for you!" He looked back at her and said, "I can't even handle Math yet, what makes you think I'm ready to handle a girlfriend?!"

Girls: "Matchmaking" is not our job! More than anything else during our teen years we need to prepare for someday being a good wife and mother. Time passes too quickly and so many times it has happened that girls get married without even knowing how to cook and clean house! It sounds unbelievable that women back then, got married at seventeen, eighteen, and nineteen years of age! But you know what? From the time they were young, they spent their time at home learning and working alongside their mothers, so when they reached eighteen, I'm sure you would agree with me, they were more than prepared for the task of raising a whole family of their own. We as girls have to be an "all-in-one" package deal for our husbands, so we will have a happy, strong, lasting marriage.

To tell you the truth cooking is not my favorite thing to do, an even though we always say we're going to marry a rich guy and be sure to hire some maids, I still say we should learn how to cook, just in case plan "A" doesn't work!

11. Christian dating robs you of having a strong, happy, future marriage.

Most problems that arise, and the main reason couples divorce in the first few years of a marriage is because of the wrong kind of seeds planted *before* the marriage. Before writing this chapter, I talked to many couples from different churches, backgrounds and walks of life, asking them this question: "Did you follow the boyfriend/girlfriend game, and what fruits did it produce for good or for bad?"

One young man said, "It produced great fruits of jealousy in me. After we married, I was jealous of any other man even talking to my wife, it also produced bitterness toward other guys. If any other fellow would have looked at my wife in the least bit, I would just as soon as killed him!"

Another one said, "By age eleven or twelve I was playing the boyfriend/girlfriend game and it caused many improper thoughts, it caused me to miss out on some normal maturity. I couldn't be a normal eleven or twelve year old because I was consumed with girls! And honestly most of it was at church. It robbed me of a lot, it cost me my friends, it caused tensions with other guys, and it created tensions in the youth group. And after I got married, it took me four years to develop the right relationship with my wife. And the reason I know was because I had gotten so used to the attention of girls, and now that I was married, I was still looking for the attention of other girls. I didn't even know why I was doing it. Parents would say to us, "Don't get serious, just date around." So I went into marriage with that same mind set. In high school I went out with a different girl and got used to the attention, I was used to flirting, and didn't know I was flirting. The dating scene had developed me to be constantly "on the prowl".

One pastor said, "Our church had activities that contributed to the boyfriend/girlfriend philosophy. The first

Monday of every month there was a skating party, it was very much in control, there was Christian music, but the whole thing catered to the boyfriend/girlfriend philosophy. The thing we all looked forward to was the "couple skate", where we could hold hands with the girl or guy we liked and skate around in a darkened rink. I know a girl and two of her brothers from an independent Baptist church, they were in church every Sunday morning, Sunday night, and Wednesday night. Today, all three of them are married and divorced twice and now living with boyfriends and girlfriends. And I know that it all went back to that boyfriend/girlfriend stuff that was in our church."

Another 20 year-old guy told me, "I had no Dad, and at age twelve I was bringing the family income. I wasn't seeking girls but by age sixteen, they were aggressively seeking me. I wanted a mate but I also wanted to serve God, it became a blurred thing. Blurred spirituality was the result in my life and, I didn't have an eye that was single towards serving God and waiting on God to bring me my life's mate. I had double vision and could not clearly see God's will for my life. I ended up backsliding and became a drunk after a girl rejected me."

Another young man said, "It produced some problems that continue until this time. It was like, getting the person of the opposite sex to like you was a game. Then when you reached the goal, you dump them and go conquer someone else. It was the very opposite of true commitment. For my wife it created a sense of feeling used and made it difficult for her to give herself to me as her mate. It created fears and distrust, and because my motives were not always pure, I was not always equipped to make her feel that she was not being used."

And yet another said, "This philosophy was definitely a reality to me. I was ten years old when I had my first girlfriend. It was so because my parents permitted it and the

"Christian" Dating

school thought it was cute. After a while, we broke up but I was hurt so badly, that as a ten year old boy, I had thoughts of suicide. The philosophy led me to do some terrible things including immorality at an early age. I had developed a sensual focus in life that caused me to think about girls continually, in the wrong way. Parents didn't interfere in this area so I developed a dangerous independent spirit, I became rebellious and ran away from home.

All of that was definitely a spin from the boyfriend/girlfriend philosophy and I still remember clearly those girls that I had strong emotions for, and it is still an uncomfortable thing for me, even after many years later, to think of running into a former girlfriend. My wife's testimony is similar to mine, this all started when back in third or fourth grade, everybody thought it was cute, it was "the way to do it". My mother especially encouraged this, she called it "growing up early", the need to be able to be independent soon. The only fruit I know of that came from this in our marriage was that we were both extremely selfish when we got married."

I will never forget one afternoon, a couple of years ago, my Dad and I were out riding our bikes when we spotted a dog crossing the road. He blindly wandered onto the freeway with a "mind-on-the-wander" expression. His tail wagged as he stepped in front of a moving car without giving it a second thought. The car slammed on its brakes, tires screamed, but the noise was deafening as the car behind it came rounding the corner and smashed right into it. The sleepy dog stopped wagging his tail for a moment and looked around at the pile of smoldering and broken cars on the freeway. His expression betrayed his thoughts. His bone-burying brain didn't equate for one moment that he was responsible for the disaster.

When a man wanders on the freeway of sin, his tail wags with delight. He thinks that this was what he was made for.

His mind wanders into lust, and suddenly a disaster sits before him. And then disaster strikes. But like that dumb dog he doesn't equate for one moment that he is solely responsible for actions. As far as he is concerned, he had a good reason for what he did. Don't be like that dumb dog! Take a look at the results of dating all around us, all the hurts, the pain, the heartache, the loss of purity, the destruction of marriages and homes! Whenever you examine the fruit of something Godly, it is always good fruit, but the fruit of dating is almost always bad fruit in some way or another. Dating is a proven failure historically and socially. In a corrupt world like the one we live in today comfort, convenience and human counsel replaces commitment, constancy and the place of the Cross in marriage. I even recently heard in the newspaper something they call a "Starter marriage". It's your first marriage where you're still trying everything out, so when you divorce and re-marry, then starts the "real" marriage because "we know how to do things better this time." That's absurd! Society argues, "If it's not fun anymore, trash it." But true love transcends emotion and remains committed.

So many times young people will prematurely give their emotions to someone who isn't God's choice for their life's mate. Guys and girls will become so-o crazy "in love" that they loose all good sense! Your emotions can get so involved that your mind and will don't function properly! You could say, "Well, now it's just emotions." But shouldn't your emotions be kept, as well, for the person you marry, if possible?

In the same way that you can develop a serious relationship with the wrong person, you can also develop a serious relationship too soon with the right person. Here's a person at fifteen or sixteen, and their dating the person who is, lets say, God's right choice for their life's mate. After about a year, they're really close and both of them *feel* like they're ready to get married. That does happen! So now what are they going to do? Are they going to get married, or are they going to break up?

Did you know that a person who doesn't *feel* like he needs to get married makes a better mate than one who feels like he just *has* to get married? Why? Because a person who just *has* to get married will sap the relationship dry, but the person who recognizes that he or she is at the point where it is God's will, and are willing to give of themselves, is more likely to build a stronger marriage. When you keep putting things *into* the marriage there will always be plenty to draw out.

It is important to realize that *worldly* dating will damage your life more than *Christian* dating will. My wild guess is that about half of all the youth playing the Christian dating game aren't being hurt too bad. It really depends on the particular standards on their Christian dating, I've put Christian dating into one huge pile here and the truth is, it's different all over the place. So whether they're being hurt or not depends on what is taken place.

But...the other half *are* being hurt and we just don't hear about it. Then there will be about ten to twenty percent of them who will really get hurt *badly*. And I'm also positive that there are many of you reading this book now, who have been, are now, or will be in that ten to twenty percent. You could say, "But hey, I played the dating game, now I'm married and everything's just fine!" But wait a minute, think. What if your son or daughter is in that ten to twenty percent?

12. Christian dating violates God's command in 2 Corinthians 5:7 that says we should "live by faith and not by sight."

Think of it this way, lets say you just met this really beautiful girl and you say, "Wow! She's the kind of girl for me! She's perfect. Yeah, I think God's just woken me up!"

Here you've just seen her outer, "Beauty Clay." But what

about her inward character? (Her family could probably tell you different!) What if she hasn't been a Christian for very long?

I may sound like your parents saying this, but don't even think of the possibility of marrying anyone who is not a strong, stable, growing Christian. I have been shocked at so many sweet, Christian guys and girls that suddenly have plans for marrying, but then all the excitement turns to disillusionment when it turns out that their husbands-to-be are *not* Christians! And you could say, "Well he's better than most Christians around here." Just talk to some women who said the same thing, now they're paying the consequences for life.

So going back to the original sentence, "we fix our eyes not on what is seen, but on that which is unseen. For what is seen is temporary, but what is unseen is eternal." -2 Corinthians 4:18

Because, "if we hope for that which we see not, then do we with patience wait for it." -Romans 8:25

This next story is a powerful testimony of what God did for a young man, and can do for you, when you "hope for" that which you can't see (your future mate), and "wait for it" with patience.

"From the time I gave my life to the Lord, back in 1973, I had the feeling that everything was going to be different and that nothing would be the same as the ways of the world, and that included the areas of dating and marriage. In this area, I felt that God, in His perfect plan for my life, was going to bring me my wife and I could just relax and wait in Him. So during this time I got busy doing the Lord's work and serving Him without distractions. I traveled a lot with teams of youth, preaching in many different cities in my country (Colombia), as well as many different countries in South America. We preached everywhere, in schools, jails, on the streets, at college campuses, and many churches and

"Christian" Dating

it was a wonderful experience. Amid all of this excitement, suddenly one morning around 3 AM., I was awakened with the feeling that I should pray for one of the girls on our outreach team that God would strengthen and encourage her heart because she was far from her family (they were in America) and serving in a country where the culture and language was totally different. After I prayed, I went back to sleep.

The next morning, the team gathered for prayer and morning devotions as usual. This girl I had prayed for told me that that night she had awakened around 3 AM., with the feeling to pray for me because I was the leader of the team and I had to take care of everything that went on during the outreaches. I just thanked her and didn't think anything about it, but it did seem unusual that she felt to pray for me at that *same* time and on that *same* night that I had felt the *same* thing. Over the next few weeks, when our team would have its morning Bible studies, we would usually share a verse of encouragement that the Lord had been speaking to us about. On three occasions, God had called my attention to meditate on certain verses. I hadn't said anything to anyone, when during the group study, this same girl would get up and share those same verses that God had given me earlier! I kept thinking these were just really great coincidences, but then after the third time, I resolved that this wasn't just a coincidence. I fell in love with Christ in her. Was God trying to wake me up? One morning, a little while later, I was praying and I asked Him if He was trying to show me something more through this, than what I was seeing. Then I felt God clearly speaking to me that she was going to be my wife. At the time, I didn't feel anything too spectacular about it but I knew that if it really was of God, He would keep on giving me clarity about the matter, confirming His will for my life in this area of marriage. At this point I wrote to my parents back in Colombia asking them to pray about this and wanting them to give me their advice about it. This girl was American and before I left Colombia to work on the mission field, one thing I remember my father told me was, "Son, I know that now you will be working with many other guys and girls from all around the world, and there is just one thing I ask of you. Please don't marry an American girl. I have two other friends who went to America and married American girls and before long, both of them became divorced. I don't want this to happen to you."

Time went on and I kept on praying without her knowing anything about this. A few weeks later, I received a letter from my parents telling me that they had prayed and fasted about it, and they felt that yes, she was the one that God had prepared to be my wife, and even though they hadn't met her in person, (they hadn't even seen a picture of her), they gave me their blessing. You would have to look the world over before you came across an American girl to marry a guy in Colombia! I lived in a small town and when the pool of candidates seemed small and hopeless, God searched my girl among the nations and He did a better job than I ever could! After that, God perfectly aligned all the circumstances and the six months later on November 19th 1979, we were swept together in what seemed like an arranged marriage-arranged by God."

Today, they live happily ever after, still actively involved doing mission work in various countries of the world, along with their small family of five. This is the story of my family. Now take time to think...if they (my parents) had chosen to reject the alternative of dating and go the dating route, then the book I wrote that you are now reading might have never been written. Had they decided they would get out from under God's authority and the authority of their parents and find their mate on their own, the story I'm telling now, would have never been told. Because many generations after also receive the consequences or the blessings of your decisions.

Give God back the pen and let Him write your love story! Don't you think He could do a better job of it anyway? He will make it something extraordinary and better than the loveliest of all fairy tales. Then it *will* be "a match made in Heaven!" So quit looking for a mate! Take care of God and he'll take care of you!

A twenty-three year old young guy said this: "I believe God has a unique plan for my life, and as part of that plan a wife He has chosen for me to love, honor, and protect as my help meet, and I can trust God to bring me the best. Why would I want to foil God's perfect plans by finding a wife in my own strength? Many young Christians are running ahead of God in regards to a spouse, instead of waiting for His best. God always comes through to us in ways we as humans cannot even fathom. And as I wait for the right one, I'll be spending my time seeking Him and His wisdom, a pastime that will always be profitable. The waiting may take some faith on my part, but God never fails."

A common complaint is, "But how will I find her if I don't date around?!" Are you living by faith or by sight? Be where you ought to be, doing what you ought to be doing, and when the time comes you'll be in just the right spot for God to bring Mr. or Mrs. Right across your path. "Seek ye first the kingdom of God and His righteousness, and *all these things* shall be added unto you." Ocupy yourself in serving God, witness, pray, win souls, and if God needs to, I can assure you that He will dump him/her right in front of you! Take life one step at a time, don't get anxious and I'll guarantee you that if you are where you ought to be, doing what you ought to be doing, you *will* get the right one!

18

And They Lived Happily Ever After…?

But why wait? Maybe you're thinking, "What?! Are you crazy? Wait instead of date? No way! That's not for me."

You're probably wondering why I am making such a big deal about this issue. One of the reasons I really want to emphasize this is because, if you think about it, all that you do and how you live your life *before* marriage determines how your life will be *after* marriage. It's the same sowing and reaping principle and works just like the law of gravity.

Statistics say that over *sixty percent* of all American children, come from broken homes, raised with a single parent. And sadly divorce rate in the church has become as common as it is in the world. That is shameful! It's devastating! But we have to take this seriously!

When will we wake up to the reality that we are now reaping the fruit of this past generation! We could tell story after story and write books and books about many broken marriages and homes of Christians, ministers, preachers, pastors, and teachers in the church. Divorce is an important and dangerous issue.

When two sheets of plywood are glued together, the wood becomes even stronger than the same thickness of wood without such bonding. Also, the bond is actually stronger than the pieces it holds together. If anyone attempts to pull the two plies of wood apart, they will permanently damage both sheets of wood. In the same way, divorce does not just damage the marriage, it does irreparable damage to both parties in the marriage.

I am tired of hearing about all the divorced, Christian couples with the excuse of "God told me to do this" and "God led me to do that." Divorce is a problem, not the solution. The sin of divorce is as bad a sin today, as it was 2,000 years ago. I remind you that the over 20th century wedding vow has always been, "Till death do us part," not "Till *divorce* do us part." The rough roads in a marriage are not so couples will run to the courts and file for a divorce because of some "irreconcilable indifferences" or because it "just didn't work out." Instead they are to cry out to God for help and realize that it is through these pressures that, if they allow Him to, God will use it mold and strengthen their relationship. The mark of a great marriage is not that it's "problem-free," but one where both partners work out their differences with sacrificial serving so that things will be better than before. I have seen it over and over again that the same problems that are not worked out in one marriage will come up in the next one and the next one no matter how many divorces, until God succeeds in getting the message across and teaching them what He wants them to learn!

As a true African proverb says, "When two elephants fight, it is the grass that suffers."

Divorced parents can find new spouses, but broken and devastated kids can't find new parents. We could talk to thousands of teens from this generation's divorced parents and they could tell you all about the pain and guilt and suffering they went through in a divorce. To say it bluntly: It has produced a generation of broken hearts.

Sam Ewing said, "Parents who wonder where the younger generation is going, should remember where it came from." Broken and devastated families. This is a fatherles generation.

I don't want to offend anyone with this but my observation is, if you are a son or daughter of divorced parents, right there you have a living example before your eyes of what could happen to you if you do not listen to the cautions our loving, heavenly Father. He clearly shows us these mistakes in the Bible so we won't blindly fall into the same whole! Scripture was written for you to avoid life's problems! (What I do is I'll read Job chapter one, and then swing across to the last chapters and say, "What did Job learn from all this, so that I can avoid the experience?") It's good to learn from your own mistakes, but it's even better to learn from others' mistakes in order to avoid them yourself. Just take a look at God's principles. They don't make sense but they sure do work!

Guys and girls, when will we wake up to this reality?! We cannot afford to give ourselves to the momentary pleasures of dating, and reap the same consequences as the generations before us! We cannot afford to make their same mistakes! It isn't enough to provide "burn clinics" for those who have been wounded or fallen—there is a desperate cry and need today to take measures and advance the means of preventative care. But the good news is, you and me can change the situation, we can do something about it! Starting with our own lives.

I think God sees us like little kids playing our little game of dating, and we think we're having fun, until it ends...but that's not *God's best*!! That's not the greatest gift He already has planned for you! You say, "But, if I don't date through my teen years, what else is there to do?! I'm not going to go through my teen years as bored as a bump on a log, because there is nothing else around here to do!" Let me tell you that the height of the stars in the sky, and the width of the earth and universe is your limit. Seek to serve the Lord without distractions! Don't wait until you're old to pursue God's best for your life! You say, "Oh but you don't know my parents!" You're right, but I *do* know our Heavenly Father, and for Him who holds the universe (and beyond!) in His hand, it is never too great for Him to give an attentive ear, and faithfully answer the cries of your heart.

You see, dating is much more than, "I like her/him and we are "going out". It's a whole life style. If each one of us really became passionate, God chasers who desperately sought after His will for our life now as young people, you would be surprised how full-filling, busy, and exciting life will be because there is no greater joy in life than to be right in the middle of God's will. And believe me, it *is* possible!

It's not about, "Oh, now I don't get to do this, I don't get to do that, I'm being cheated!

I'm being robbed of the best part of my youth!" Oh, come on! If that's the way you live your whole Christian life, you're going to be the most miserable person that ever walked the face of this planet! But, if you catch the spirit of it... "Hey, I don't have to worry about it anymore, I don't have to be on the prowl, I don't have to defraud or deceive anyone, I don't have to walk into marriage with a defiled conscience, or any extra baggage, I can be free! Yeah! That's the way to do it!" Then you're going to be one happy Christian!

The next time your friends say, "What? You're not dating?!" Say, "You mean you *are*?!"

One of the hardest things you can ever do in life is to go against the current. If you've already gotten involved, it will be tough to turn back; but always remember, you can do anything when God is backing you up, because He will empower you! The waiting isn't easy, but it's right and it's the best! Don't burn up the years of your youth, have high goals and standards now! Live it so you can look back later on in life and say, " I did something great with my life, I don't have any regrets."

You say, "But hey, *everyone* is doing it." Not me! When I grow up some day I want to get married, and I want to have a big family, a *big* family (ten kids at least!) who grow up to serve God and do great things for Him with their lives. But more than all of this, I want to be able to stand at the altar on my wedding day and give away my *whole* heart to my darling husband, not the extra, left-over pieces, but the *whole* thing. And I want my marriage to stand out as a living testimony that this *is* possible, and it is the best!

I once saw a billboard which was an advertisement and it showed a whole bunch of little paper cups turned upside down on a beach. There was a man standing beside them, looking down upon all those paper cups, then the sign said, "Your right mortgage is under one of these cups. Get-A-Home will help you find it." I was just thinking how this very same commercial could apply in this area. "Your right "mate" is under one of these cups. Only Christ will help you find it."

So what's the solution? Truth is simple. I can say it all in seven words, "Go to sleep and wait on God!" Sleep, but from the dating spirit, get busy soul-winning, serving and sowing seed that you will look forward to reaping after. Wait until it is time and God will wake you up with this surprise He has been preparing and waiting to show you since you were born!

It's too simple. Love is a wonderful and unique thing, and it lasts forever when it's done the right way...God's way. Then you can be free to talk to all guys and girls the same, and have friends, and be yourself, without having to worry about anything.

But don't just take this because you read it from this book, instead because you just discovered it, from God for yourself. Even more, make sure you get the *spirit* of all this and not just the letter; "for the letter kills, but the Spirit gives life." —2 Corinthians 3:6

People tell me, "Sounds nice, but this waiting thing just doesn't work for me." That's just like the people who say, "Oh I tried Christianity but it didn't work for me." It's because they treat it as a formula. It's not about rules and regulations or formulas to make it "safer". It's about a change in mindset! You have to wake up and realize the beauty of pursuing a relationship God's way and in God's timing. You have to start focusing on the heart of the issue. Don't plug in the different steps of the formula, seek God and you will know. *Anybody can get married, but it takes a special, "God-picked" person to really make it work.* And you won't find him/her in the newspaper or on the internet.

(Sorry guys, the following analogy may relate more to the girls, but maybe you can think of something!)

I have a collection of perfumes from places all over the world in every color, shape, size and scent. Perfumes are categorized by their rarity, cost and sweet smell. In a store, the more valuable ones are placed up on a shelf, locked behind glass doors. Customers can come in to see, touch, and try on all the cheaper brands, which are found on shelves that are in reach, but not this precious beauty behind the glass doors. No...she is reserved for only one. She stays there until some day one customer will come, see her value, and purchase it, no matter the cost.

Give yourself the value of that precious perfume. You determine your worth in the way you see yourself and let others treat you. You can't settle to be on the cheap rack whith those who are popular and numerous. You have to be like that one rare beauty, saved for only one. And when you feel like your parents are too strict and "lock you in," thank them for it!

Give the key of the glass doors of your heart to your Dad, and on that beautiful day, when the customer will walk in...your Dad can then give him the key to your heart and...you can finish the story.

If there is anything I want you to remember from this whole topic, it is this analogy I just told. Because if you can just give yourself the value of something like this, then you will be able to wait and save your whole heart.

Have you ever walked along the sandy shores of a beach at night when the silvery moon is full, and its light beautifully reflects on the calm waters. That is very romantic, and God created it all that way. God is the Great Romanticist, He created love and romance. But this great romance is not what we are used to feeling, that kind of "love" where you get sweaty palms, a loud heart throb or a bunch of butterflies in your stomach fluttering around and crashing into each other! It's so much more than that! It's a love that is "stronger than death", a love that "no waters can quench". Because God's love and romance is so great, it lasts forever. One of the best things you can do to encourage yourself, when you see all your friends playing the dating game, and you start to feel lonely and wonder if your mate for life will really be worth all this waiting, (sometimes it's *really* hard to stay asleep!).

Think about the future. Time will tell. There is no substitute for waiting and you will never be sorry that you did however long you had to. Remember who you're waiting for, and remember that every emotion and every piece of your heart that you save for your future mate, will someday be like a cord that will make a stronger bond in uniting your future marriage.

So I encourage you with all my heart, don't eat the cake before the party!

19

Wounds from a Friend or Kisses from an Enemy?

"**F**aithful are the wounds of a friend; but the kisses of a enemy are deceitful."—Proverbs 27:6 KJV

One of the most powerful forces in the universe, outside of God, are human relationships. Your relationships are the key to your personal success or failure; they will either coach you you're your destiny or distract and "restrict" you from your ultimate purpose. In fact after thinking about it for a while, everything that you do today, good or bad, is a product of the people you know and spend time with, and the lessons you've learned through it.

George Washington once said, "Be courteous to all, but intimate with few, and let those few be well tried before you give them your confidence. True friendship is a plant of slow growth and must undergo and withstand the shocks of adversity before it is entitled to appellation."

For most of us, friends make up a big part of our lives, and the type of friends you choose is what determines the outcome of your life. Your friends will lead you (unless you are the leader yourself) the right way or the wrong way, and hold the potential to hinder your spiritual growth and maturity. Wrong friends aren't necessarily comprised of evil people. Many times they are just normal, good people who are also trapped in relationships that are simply not right for them.

Proverbs 12: 26 says that, "The righteous is more excellent than his neighbor: but the way of the wicked seduceth him."

When you don't participate in all their invitations, your friends will make you feel like you have missed our on the greatest thing, but believe me you haven't! They are just so caught up in their momentary, empty pleasures that they can't begin to imagine that anything else at that moment could be greater. It's as if they keep looking through a tube, they love what they see on the other side, but they don't just get their face out to see they could be a part of the whole picture. Friends can leave you and forsake you, but when you go to Jesus, you can find in Him a friend that sticks closer than a brother.

When you take a shower and you turn on the knob of hot and cold water, what do you get? Right, warm water. *Lukewarm* water. That's just how we can become luke-warm Christians. When we have the imbalance of letting others wrongly influence us, instead of leaning on the hot side, with mature Christian friends that are in the same spirit and will challenge us up in our walk with the Lord. Unfortunately, there are not very many of those kinds of friends. Remember, we are to be *in* the world but not *of* it. We have friends in the world, but we aren't one of them.

Sadly lukewarmness in today's Christians has become like a highly contagious epidemic that is spreading far and wide and is slowly destroying the body of Christ. That's why I want to talk about this because it happens primarily through relationships.

Lukewarmness comes when we stop looking to Jesus as our standard, perfect example and role model, and we start comparing ourselves with other Christians, looking to them for measuring our standards of what is right and wrong. There is a great danger about that because when we do that, we will tend to become mediocre, because we find ourselves between two standards: those who are passionate, "Christ-like" Christians, and those who are more-less, carnal Christians; those who are the best Christians and those who are the worst Christians. Remember the first chapter in this book where we talked about comparing ourselves to a standard of Hitler and Maria Theresa? You can compare yourself with others and you may fare well, but when you compare yourself to the true 'standard' which is Jesus Christ, we all "fall short."

But we can't settle to be mediocre Christians! This word "mediocre" comes from the Latin root *mediocris,* meaning "half way up the mountain." You can't be a "half-way-up-the-mountain" Christian, you have to go all the way!

Spiritual defeat in a Christian's life doesn't happen all at once, it is usually the result of subtle, permeating influences that first rob us of our love and passion for God, and then we are drawn away by the false philosophies that the world filters into our minds. As our love for God decreases, so does the "savor" of our salt and our spiritual strength.

The Bible uses the term "lukewarm" many times to describe our spiritual condition, and one of these occasions He wanted to teach us a lesson using the church in Laodicea. Laodicea was a place which attracted many wealthy people as a center for ease and retirement, because of it's ideal climate and very strategic location. Everything was perfect except it had one disadvantage: it lacked a permanent supply of good water. The residents tried to solve the problem by constructing a long, stone pipe to hot springs close by, except when the water reached Laodicea, it was lukewarm. Showing their disgust and disappointment, the townspeople took a mouthful of water and spit it out on the ground. Jesus knew exactly how to get his message across about lukewarmness and that's why he said, "I know thy works, that thou art neither hot nor cold: I wish you were one or another!

So then because thou art lukewarm, and neither cold nor hot, I will spew thee out of my mouth." -Revelations 3:15-16

In his book entitled "Confession", Leo Tolstoy perfectly describes this concept of lukewarmness in the following: "A certain intelligent and honest man named S. once told me of how he ceased to be a believer. At the age of twenty-six, while taking shelter for the night during a hunting trip, he knelt to pray in the evening as had been his custom since childhood. His older brother, who had accompanied him on the trip, was lying down on some straw and watching him. When S. had finished and was getting ready to lie down, his brother said to him, "So you still do that." And they said nothing more to each other. From that day S. gave up praying and going to church. And for thirty years he has not prayed, he has not taken holy communion, and he has not gone to church, not because he shared his brother's convictions and went along with them; nor was it because he had decided on something or other in his own soul. *It was simply that the remark his brother had made, was like the nudge of a finger against a wall that was about to fall over from its own weight.* His brother's remark showed him that the place where he thought faith to be had long since been empty; subsequently the words he had spoke, the signs of the cross he had made, and the bowing of his head in prayer were in essence completely meaningless actions." (p.15-16)

"But it is happened to them according to the true proverb, The dog is returned to his own vomit again and;

and the sow that was washed, to her wallowing in the mire." —2 Peter 2:22 Don't be a fool and return to your vomit!

Losing our love and passion for God is a result of something, not a cause of something.

In the same way that salt loses its savor, when it is mixed with other impure elements, we as Christians will loose our effectiveness when we allow ourselves to be contaminated with the world, which is the lust of the flesh, the lust of the eyes, and the pride of life. "Because of the increase of wickedness, the love of most will grow cold, but he who stands firm to the end will be saved." —Matthew 24:12-13

Over and over all through the Bible I have noticed, from the Old Testament to the New, the one thing God speaks to us, that never changes and is depicted in different ways, such as stories parables, teachings, and preachings is, "go back to your first love." It is so easy for us to forget and loose our first love. And God compares that to an adulterating woman, who has left the husband of her youth, and gone off with other strangers. It's something that has already been a problem since the beginning of days, yet it is still a dangerous reality. For me or you to turn our backs on God now, would be to turn back on the greatest thing that ever happened in your life, and could ever happen to you.

Seriously I have been very shocked at the quality of Christianity today's youth are living. It is so diluted! It's absurd! I have realized that, anymore, the label "Christian" doesn't mean the same as it did fifty years ago. That's why Jesus says in Matthew 7:15-20, "Ye shall know them by their fruits. Do men gather grapes of thorns, or figs of thistles? Even so every good tree bringeth forth good fruit; but a corrupt tree bringeth forth evil fruit... Wherefore by their fruits ye shall know them."

Matthew 5:13 says, "Ye are the salt of the earth but if the salt has lost its savor wherewith shall it be salted? It is thenceforth good for nothing but to be cast out and to be trodden under foot of men." And in my paraphrased version: You are the salt of the earth, but if you loose your savor and effectiveness, how will you be re-savored? Un-savored salt is good for nothing except to be thrown out and destroyed."

In the Greek concordance that word "salt" is translated "prudence". So if we would write it in the original Greek it would sound more like, "ye are the *prudence* of the earth." We have to keep the earth from rotting and going bad! We have to be savory salt. When savory salt is spread on meat, it keeps the bacteria from spoiling the meat. In the same way, Christians are to stop the spread of evil from destroying our country, by being that savory salt and light. Something's wrong with the savor of our salt! In recent years of church history, men have been looking for better *methods*, while God has been looking for better *men*.

Edmund Burke said, "The only thing necessary for the triumph of evil is for good men to do nothing."

One of the most common questions people ask about God is "How can He be such a loving God and there be so much evil in the world?" I'll tell you why, its because we as Christians aren't doing our job of stopping the spread of evil in this world!

In Bible times, unsavory salt was thrown out on the road to be trampled on. In the same way, unsavory Christians will allow evil to be the major influence in government and then the result is a corrupt law system which will then take freedom from Christians and bring them "to be trodden under foot". Think of America back in the 1940's. Problems in society were much different than today. School trouble was: talking, chewing gum, making noise, running in the hall, getting out of turn in line, wearing improper clothing, and not putting paper in the trash.

Today, after someone thought it would be a good idea to take the Ten Commandments and prayer out of school, listen to the problems in American schools. Rape, robbery, assault, bombings, murder, suicide, vandalism, extortion, alcohol and drug abuse, gang warfare, pregnancies, abortions, and now you can add homosexuality and AIDS to that list.

And the worst part of all this is that we as Christians just sit back and kind of get used to letting it all happen. This is not a time to sit back and relax! This is not a time to get all down and discouraged because of all this! It's time to stand up, clean up your armor, and pick up your sward and charge into battle claiming the victory! Satan is putting up a big fight for today's youth, and anymore he doesn't care how old or young they could be, because he knows that the future of any church, city, state, country, and consequently the next generation, is in the lives and decisions of today's youth.

Do you realize that even a few "salty" Christians are enough to preserve and save a whole nation! God does not destroy a nation for the sins of the wicked as much as for the ineffectiveness of the righteous! Take Sodom and Gomorrah for example. If Lot had just discipled his own family and a few neighbors, the cities would have been spared. Instead, he spent much time and energy just worrying about the filthy deeds of the wicked people (without doing much about it) and lost most of his own family.

When salt is spread on meat, it keeps the bacteria from spoiling the meat. In the same way, Christians are supposed to spread out to stop the spread of evil in our countries, by being strong salt and light! People who eat salt always become thirsty, it's a fact. I remember seeing a really awesome Christian T-shirt that said, "So if you're really salt, have you made anyone thirsty yet?" People who are around "salty" Christians should begin to hunger and thirst after God. Be such a strong, 'salty' Christian, and live your life in such a way that everyone will come thirsting after what you've got!

Like my grandpa always says, "You can't ride both sides of the fence." You might have a lot of fun, and get a lot of laughs, but you won't impact as many people and you will just stay shallow and empty in your Christianity. You'll completely miss the mark and you will eventually burn out on it. Just as a lamp needs oil to make it shine, we need the Holy Spirit to live in our hearts and have the Bible to be our guide so that as we are constantly taking in the oil, we will always have something inside to power the brightness of the light we shine.

We are the source of light of this world and God expects us to light and re-light other Christians. We need to constantly fill our lives with the "Jesus oil".

Christianity isn't for wimps. There are two types of people on this earth, those who influence and those who are influenced, those who lead and those who follow. The history makers and world shakers, or the "coward, lukewarm Christians." Which kind are you? Truly happy and successful people know who they are in the Lord, and where they are going. they are the leaders, opinion makers, and trendsetters, and they strive confidently to meet their goals. Be an "influencer" and leader! Those are the people who really make something out of themselves in life.

A father and son once went on a camping trip. When they arrived at the sight, the father pitched the tent and said, "Son, see that river over there, it's full of crocodiles. So if you want to do any fishing, fish off the bridge." The son says, "Ok Dad, I'll fish off the bridge."

For three days the kid fished off the bridge, and after a while, it began to get kind of boring. He began thinking, "You know, I'll be safe in a boat among the crocodiles, in fact, it might be kind of exciting out there." So he got a boat, went out into the river full of crocodiles and began fishing.

Things were sweet for a time, until one crocodile came alongside that boat and its tail swung and hit the boat and overturned it. The kid screamed in terror and the father heard his scream, and without hesitation dived of the edge of the bridge and into the dark, crocodile infested waters. He grabbed his beloved son and pulled him to the safety of the shore. But when the son opened his eyes, he saw a horrific sight. A crocodile had just wrapped his massive jaws around his father's legs, leaving him in bleeding shreds.

What I am about to say now is unthinkable, but imagine if that son looked at his father lying there in agony, bleeding to death, and said something like this, "Dad, I really appreciate what you've just done for me. But you know, I found it kind of exciting out there amongst the crocodiles—you wouldn't mind if I get into the boat and go out again, would you?"

If that son could think such a thing, let alone speak it, the blind fool hasn't seen the sacrifice his father has just made for him! Because if that son has truly seen what his father has just done for him, a sense of horror will consume him at the cost, the extreme, the length, the expense his father went to, to save him. He will pour contempt over the very drops of blood that's still cling to his flesh.

Dear professing Christian, if you have any hidden desire to go back into the sinful excitement of the world, you haven't realized the extent of the sacrifice of your Father. No one else may know-but you know, Satan knows, and God knows when deep in your heart there is a yearning to go back into the world. A wise man once said, "Many persons who appear to repent are like sailors who throw their goods overboard in a storm, and then wish for them again in calm."

The true Christian who has seen how, without hesitation, Jesus Christ dived into the very jaws of Hell to save him from the foolishness and destruction of sin. A sense of horror would consume him at the cost, the extreme, the length, and the expense his Father went to, to save him, and he pours contempt upon the sinful desires that still cling to his flesh.

An overwhelming sense of gratitude should engulf you that your Savior bled on the cross for your sins, and that should be your prime motivation to serve God and push you to evangelize. When our Christian life seems like a dry and lifeless sermon without end, and the joy of feeding on God's Word is no longer in our hearts, we must get on our knees and return to our first love.

20

Taking Up the Martyrs' Torch Once Again

"A few years ago in Kiangsi, China, two, young, Christian girls and their pastor were sentenced to death. As on many such occasions in church history, the persecutors mocked and scorned them for being so foolish as to die for an unseen God. Then they promised the pastor that if he would shoot the girls, they would release him. He accepted.

The girls waited patiently in their prison cells for the moment of their execution. They prayed quietly together. Soon the guards came for them and led them out. A fellow prisoner who watched the execution through the barred walls of his prison cell, said that their faces were pale but beautiful beyond belief, infinitely sad but sweet. They were placed against a wall, and their pastor was brought forward by two guards. They placed him close in front of the girls and put a pistol into his hand.

The girls whispered to each other, then bowed respectfully to their pastor. One of them said, "Before being shot by you, we wish to thank you heartily for what you have meant to us. You baptized us, you taught us the way of eternal life, you gave us Holy Communion with the same hand in which you now have a gun. May God also reward you for all that you have done for us. You also taught us that Christians are sometimes weak and commit terrible sins, but they can be forgiven again. When you regret what you are about to do to us, do not despair like Judas, but repent like Peter. God bless you, and remember that our last thought of you was not one of indignation against your failure. Everyone passes through hours of darkness. We die with gratitude." (Foxes Book of Martyrs" (pp. 339-340)

Witnessing has never been so easy, and even today many believers face death and still share God's word. Compared to that, today we hold back because someone might laugh! What have we done to repay Christ for what He did for us on the Cross? Where have we placed that great value of our faith?

2 Timothy 3:12 says, "...all that will live godly in Christ Jesus shall suffer persecution."

It doesn't say "might suffer", it says "*All...will* suffer". We can see many, many examples of this in the Bible. Joseph listened to God and he got in trouble. Daniel listened to God and he got into trouble. Moses listened to God and he got into trouble. *Jesus* listened to God and he got into *big* trouble! In fact he was murdered for it. It's a fact! Everyone who really listens and obeys God, gets into big trouble! So know that if you ever listen to God and obey what He says, you *will* get into big trouble. But every grain of wheat has to die to self before it can be useful and fruitful.

You can read all about great revolutionary preachers and teachers who gave their lives until death to serve Christ and expand His kingdom here on earth. They went through all kinds of torture and none of it caused them to coward back or slow down with their witness. I have studied the lives of ancient martyrs and those of modern times, and one thing that disheartens me of the modern-day church is the testimonies of so many Christians who turned back on their faith and denied Jesus with the hope or "promise" of reduced suffering or release.

Mathew 5:11 says to "Rejoice and be exceedingly glad when men shall revile you and persecute you and say all manner of evil against you falsely for my sake." Most of the time this verse has been taken in the context of persecution like many Christians are experiencing today in many countries where the gospel is "prohibited." But we can take this verse for situations we face every day too.

My paraphrased version says, "Rejoice and get excited when others laugh at you, mock you, stare at you, gossip about you in a false way, and call you a "geek", "wierdo", "holier-that-thou" or "saint" for My sake. For then you'll have a greater reward in heaven!"

A number of years ago when Russia was in severe persecution against Christians, I heard there was a prayer meeting among a number of Christians. Suddenly the doors burst open and two, fully armed Russian soldiers yelled, "Get out of this place if you're not willing to die for your faith!"

Half of all those professing Christians jumped up and ran for their lives. Then when the doors closed, the guards put down their guns, took of their hats, sat down and said, "Praise God, were just sorting out the sheep from the goats before they risk fellowship!"

Christianity in modern day believers has become so diluted! We have become "throwaway, trashy, disposable Christians!" We go to church one Sunday and then miss the next because we're mad at someone, or the pews were uncomfortable. We question God for every little trial and tribulation that comes along and we get discouraged when circumstances don't go our way. You see, if we had more persecution, what it would do is it would rid the church of murmurs and complainers, and strengthen true conversions. Think of a plant. If you want it to grow, you need good soil, a lot of water and plenty of sunlight, am I right? So the worst thing you and I can do for a plant is to shelter it from the sunlight. In the same way, the worst thing you and I can do to a new believer, is shelter them from persecution. Because if he is genuine, he will grow. If he is false, he will wither up and die.

More than any other generation before us, we are closer to the Age of the Anti-Christ and the second coming of Jesus. Will we be ready? Will we stand strong in the face of adversity? How long and how much we willing to suffer torture, ridicule, cold, humiliation, starvation and death, for the cause of Christ? In these latter days the unyielding truth may cause us to have to pay the ultimate price for our faith. When the fire gets hot and the furnace is turned up, that's when you can *really* see what you're made of and what's really inside of you.

Remember the story about when Gideon sounded his trumpet to call all those to battle? 32,000 men volunteered to fight against their enemy of 135,000. However, God had a different plan which didn't require 32,000. In Deuteronomy 20:8, according to the Mosaic Law it was commanded that, "Is there any man afraid or fainthearted? Let him go home so that his brothers will not become disheartened too." So God "purified" this group of men until there were only 300 left. When looking forward to battle, the last thing that Gideon expected God to do was cut down his army. Why would God do that? To fight a battle of 135,000 enemies with only 300 men is what I call absolutely impossible! But Gideon's small band of 300 perfectly obeyed God's battle plans and defeated the Midianites, without one single man in his army being killed! Even when the ratio was four to one and Gideon's army couldn't stand a chance to win no matter what, the God of the impossible doesn't have limitations, unless you put the limitations. "Behold, I am the Lord the God of all flesh: is there anything too hard for me?" —Jeremiah 32:27

The world is tired of false people. People are sick and disgusted with just professing religion. They are tired of sitting in a pew, listening to sermons, and never going out during the week to win anyone to the Lord, and the church is dying because of it. I think God wants to cleanse us so that the only ones that are left to transform this world and impact this generation, are those who are really "hot" and truly on fire for God and willing to give it all for Him.

John Wycliffe said, "Faith is likened to the corn of seed. If the corn of seed be not broken, the virtue thereof is not known; but the more it is pounded, even the stronger it smelleth; even so a man who is firmly grounded in his faith, the more he is pounded by persecution, the greater and the more fervent is his belief."

So I'm telling you, if you *are* doing anything worthwhile for God, you *will* be persecuted! You should be hated and despised! Satan will try to trample you to the ground!

Jesus told us that over two thousand years ago! The world hated Him, so if you and Jesus have anything in common, the world will hate you! If you are not getting very much opposition or persecution, start worrying! Because it might be that you're probably not doing very much to threaten the kingdom of darkness either.

I know that in America you would have to be making lot of scandal with the gospel to get any persecution at all. One evangelist said, "I've stood up and preached open-air over three thousand times. And in all that time, once I had a can of Coke poured down my back on a hot day, so actually it was quite pleasant. A lot of verbal abuse, a couple of stones thrown at me here and there, a few tin cans. Once someone took a hot french-fry and threw it at me while I was preaching, and by the grace of God I was able to catch it, eat it, and keep on preaching. Then I saw another one coming and grabbed it, but it was the end of a hot cigarette!"

I think true persecution is something we need more of in America. Persecution is part of what shows the difference between a true or false conversion! I know it would be a shocking wake up call for all of us, but we need it. William Penn said, "No pain, no palm; no thorns, no throne; no gall, no glory; no cross, no crown."

Remember that during persecution, you can turn every problem that comes your way, into a stepping stone rather than a stumbling block. That's why the apostle Paul rejoiced in suffering for Christ. He was no happy-clappy, superficial Christian. He knew that every scar on his flesh was a testimony of a deeper commitment to His Savior. Every stripe across his back with the whip, not only revealed a heart sold out to God, but it cut a fresh resolve in his soul to further die to this world and live for the next.

Leonard Ravenhill, many years ago said these words about communism that have proved so true, "My head hangs low that communists would give more for their dying cause, than we will give for the living Christ." So many times we give ourselves to without reserve to deathly causes, but you and I as Christians, we've got a cause that's worth suffering and dying for. So why are we scared to witness? Why are we fearful to preach?

And I am convinced that it's only a fear of rejection, that's all it is. Its not a fear of getting our blood spilled! Perfect loves casts out all fear!

When John Wesley was still young, he and a group of some other young men would get together to study and talk about the scriptures. Others laughed at them and called their group the "Holy Club". (Kind of sounds like something others would call a cell group or discipleship group today.)

But you know something that has gotten my attention with this group of the "Holy Club"? Everywhere you read about John Wesley, you never hear about the others who were making fun of them, their names aren't even mentioned in the history books! Nevertheless, their group (John and Charles Wesley, George Whitefield, Jonathan Edwards and many others), they were the ones who truly impacted England and started a revival which later spread throughout Europe and turned the world upside down.

21

Catch the Vision!

A few months ago I received an email. It said that the following was written on a piece of scrap paper by an African pastor the night before some rebels murdered him because he refused to denounce his faith. I want you to read this slowly and let his words sink down deep into your heart.

"I am a part of the "Fellowship of the Unashamed". I have Holy Spirit power. The dye has been cast. I've stepped over the line. The decision has been made. I am a disciple of His. I won't look back, let up, slow down, back away, or be still. My past is redeemed, my present makes sense, and my future is secure. I am finished and done with low living, sight walking, small planning, smooth knees, colorless dreams, tame visions, mundane talking, chintzy giving, and dwarfed goals!

I no longer need preeminence, prosperity, position, promotions, plaudits, or popularity. I don't have to be right, first, tops, recognized, praised, regarded, or rewarded. I now live by the presence, learn by faith, love by patience, lift by prayer, and labor by power.

My face is set, my gait is fast, my goal is Heaven, my road is narrow, my way is rough, my companions few, my Guide reliable, my mission clear. I cannot be bought, compromised, detoured, lured away, turned back, diluted, or delayed.

I will not flinch in the face of sacrifice, hesitate in the presence of adversity, negotiate at the table of the enemy, ponder at the pool of popularity, or meander in the maze of mediocrity. I won't give up, shut up, let up, or burn up, till I've preached up, prayed up, paid up, stored up, and stayed up for the cause of Christ. I am a disciple of Jesus. I must go till He comes, give till I drop, preach till all know, and work till He stops. And when He comes to get His own, He'll have no problems recognizing me. My colors will be clear."

Wow! Talk about being sold out for God. As I read the above story, I could just sense this pastor's passion for Jesus. I want that kind of passion! We have to not only be willing to die for Him but also willing to *live* completely sold out for Him. We are living in a time where people want things to be real. They are tired of hypocrisy. Like it says on a Coke can with less sugar; it's a diet drink. It says, "Coke *'light'* 12 fluid oz. We have been living a *"light"* Christianity and things have to change because anymore, life is not like in Bible times. Quit playing church and surrender yourself totally to God and His plan for your life!

A very wise man once said, "We must out-love, out-serve, and out-sacrifice any others who claim to have a way to solve life's problems." This is the only way we can ever expect to be salt and light of this earth. This is the only way we can fulfill the mission of reaching the ends of the earth. We're quickly approaching the end of times and we have to get desperate to see God bring a total transformation to our lives, so we can then change the world for Christ! Our priority as youth in this new millennium is get our life straight and spread the salvation message as fast as we possibly can because our time is running out. There is no longer a place for us to live halfway Christian lives. I want to challenge you to find what this pastor had: a total sold out, passionate heart for God!

"And they that be of thee shall build of old waste places: thou shalt raise up the foundations of many generations; and thou shalt be called, The repairer of the breach, The restorer of paths to dwell in." —Isaiah 58:12 KJV

Each one of us have been called to raise up the foundations of the next generation and "repair the breach" in healing the lives of all those who are hurt and dying in this lost world. We are chosen to restore the ancient paths, which our Christian forefathers laid, but have been destroyed and lost, by the past generations.

"They would not be like their forefathers—a stubborn and rebellious generation, whose +hearts were not loyal to God, whose spirits were not faithful to him." —Psalm 78:8

We have to be different than all the other generations before us who didn't serve God. We have to take responsibility and authority to raise the standard and lead and change the sinful, lost direction to which our generation is heading. The youth of today have received many, many prophecies of all the ways God is wanting to use us and all the awesome things He wants to use do through us to further extend His kingdom, but it won't just suddenly start happening. It is up to us, you and me, to step out in faith, get moving and make it happen! If and when we do our part, He'll be sure to take care of the rest!

We have to be the "Joshuas" and "Calebs" to bring back the "good report" of our potential as Christians in impacting other nations for Christ, walking through the land to claim it for Christ. Think. When was the last time that you did something for God that was humanly "illogical"? Let's not be like the ten timid spies, who preferred the false security and comfort of the wilderness, over the uncomfortable risks of conquest. Cry out for God to chase you for the rest of your life, and never again let you get into your comfort zone. Your comfort zone is one of the most dangerous places you can be. We are too fat, too secure and too passive! Everything God has for you is out of the boat. All of life is about pushing out of your comfort zone. You can stay in your comfort zone, but you won't grow and you won't be the very best you can be in everything you do. Don't let another young person go to Hell because you're too comfortable. A container of water that isn't being continually changed will get stagnant and spoil its usefulness. We need to have our comfortable lives destroyed by the Holy Spirit, as He brings an authentic "death" to our lives and makes room for His true light.

Christians everywhere are frail and broken. When we humble ourselves before God and give Him our weaknesses, He has a chance to become strong through us and continue perfecting us through His mercy. It is in this way that the Holy Spirit moves in each one of us, and as He moves in us, so He moves in the world. If you make yourself available, He will increase your vitality and show you how to use your resources to further His kingdom here on earth. Every minute of our life is precious, and our ability to run this race of life only comes from God as we recognize our incapability and daily cry out to Him for direction. Without Jesus Christ you and I can do nothing. Nothing can produce good fruit on its own, it always needs and depends on someone or something else. God chose you and me, that we may always be attached to Him so that the fruit that we produce will be good fruit…fruit that lasts forever. We can be producing fruit even while we're young.

There was a young man who grew up and lived in the city of Macedonia, Greece. At the age of thirteen, he became a pupil of the great Greek philosopher, Aristotle, who was

Catch the Vision!

brought from the city of Athens specifically to be his tutor. Under Aristotle's tutelage, his love for Hellenic culture was reinforced as he, like many other young boys of his day, memorized Homer's *Iliad*. He even came to see himself as the second Achilles, the great Greek war-hero of the *Iliad*, and he resolved to use his conquests to spread the Greek Hellenic culture all around the world.

He was twenty years old and quite prepared to take up his father's throne, since he had been trained in his father's army and had proved himself to be a fearless, valiant warrior and an able leader. In 334 B.C., he crossed Hellespoint to begin his conquest of the mighty Persian Empire. Along with some other 35,000 Greek and Macedonian soldiers, his army included engineers, surveyors and others whose job was constructing war engines and plans for their strategy of attacks. After defeating the Persian forces at the Granicus River and at Issus in Asia Minor, quickly he subdued all of Syria, Palestine, and Egypt. Shortly after that, he captured Babylon, Susa and Persepolis, wealthy cities which gave him rich treasures. After the death of Darius 3rd, at the hands of his own army, he became the official ruler of Persia and soon the whole Persian Empire was his. He charged into battle like a goat with a single, powerful horn-trampling everything in his path. He conquered the whole eastern Mediterranean world.

You've probably already guessed it, but this is the story of a young man named Alexander the Great. Alexander started his quest at age twenty, and his life ended with a fever which he got at age thirty-three. My point in telling you this story is to say, Alexander the Great was no "Greek Superman"! He just had the initiative and determination to aspire unto greatness while he was really young!

History records that David was anointed king of Israel at age fifteen. Mozart composed his first symphony at age six. Joan of Arc led 3,000 French Knights to victory in the Battle of Orleans when she was just seventeen. Einstein wrote his first paper on the theory of relativity when he was sixteen. They stepped out of normality! They hit the mark!

 A secret but powerful weapon the enemy loves to use against us to keep us from doing great things for God, is a small ambition called "normality". We want to be "normal" Christians, "normal" people. There is a great pull to normality in our world today. As Christians we no longer aspire unto great things as did other great Christians before us. The typical greatness in life we have become so used to is: growing up, making "good" grades in school, studying at a "great" university, pursuing a "high" degree, getting married, raising "good" kids, oh, and we almost forgot to mention, going to church. Then the whole cycle starts all over again with the next generation. It's such a bizarre thing because in our world today we have such small ambitions that blind us, take up all our time, and blur our focus of having greater ambitions in life! We have gotten so accustomed to living a "normal" Christian life, and yet Jesus, and spreading His Word unto the ends of this earth is sadly seldom our main focus in life. One of our greatest enemies in life are these small ambitions that take our eyes off that great calling that God has for our lives and causes us to look down as animals on the small ambitions in life. Those small ambitions that take up all our time but in the end, when we look back, we see that there is really nothing we have accomplished, there is no lasting fruit. If we're going to have high ambitions in life and learn to ignore the smaller ones, we have to start seeing things as God sees them. So many times we find ourselves battling with small issues in this life and we feel like we should just give up, and in a way we should. Give up all your small ambitions! Give it *all* up, give God back first place in your life, and let Him be the strong one in your weaknesses.

 David Livingston said, "I have found that I have no unusual endowments of intellect, but I this day resolved that

I would be an uncommon Christian."

This world needs young guys and girls who are totally given over and sold out to Him, and better yet, whole families that aspire unto greatness and be the outstanding examples that this lost and dying world needs. Sadly, most Christian families are so busy working, studying, making money, raising a family, and using up all their time and energy battling with the world, just trying to keep their teens in church, and on the right track, that they don't have the time and energy to move on to greater things!

Jesus tells us "seek ye *first* the kingdom of God and His righteousness and *all these things* will be added." I couldn't paraphrase this verse more clearly! We are actually doing things the hard way because we are seeking all these things first and then expecting the kingdom of God to be added. But it's the wrong way! We have left out the most important ingredient of all. It's about living a "kingdom-focused" life.

When I say "aspire unto greatness" I mean this. Have you ever written a book, booklet or even a pamphlet that could give practical help or inspiration to other people? How many Christian youth today have become great authors, preachers, teachers, evangelists, or even great, Godly presidents of a country? Is Abraham Lincoln the first and only example we see of a godly man who born in a log cabin, aspired to greatness?! And it was all because he "sought the kingdom of God first" and set his mind to do it! Speaking worldwide, how many God-fearing men and presidents have there been throughout history compared to those that are not God-fearing and have become great? It almost seems as though people of the secular world do aspire unto greater things than most Christians!

I don't believe that anyone is conceived in the womb and born into this world as an accident or without a purpose. Will you be another George Whitefield and start a third Great Awakening we so desperately need? Will you be mother to a future president of your country? Will you be the next C.S. Lewis, Ludwig von Beethoven, Winston Churchill or Leonardo DaVinci? Yes you could. Because God has given you that same potential.

Have you ever prayed and asked God, "Please direct my paths so I can know in what way I can effectively do the greatest good to the greatest number of people." If not, what are you waiting for?! Don't wait until you get old to catch the vision and do something great for God with your life. Start now! Don't let the world distract you!

There more to life than what you are experiencing right now. There is more to life than spending your time watching life in a box (TV)! Get out and live it…the right way! Take a look outside the box! We tend to be very narrow minded in our way of thinking about life. Our perspective of the world is like looking at it through a tube, God is the only one who really sees the whole picture. God has got more behind our backs than we could ever see in front of our faces! God's best, in every aspect of life, is waiting for you-and He doesn't want you to settle for anything less. Don't burn up the years of your youth, have high goals and standards now! Live it so you can look back later on in life and say, " I did something great with my life and I don't have any regrets."

As Lawrence of Arabian once said, "Not dreamers of the night dreaming in the dusty recesses of our mind, but dreamers of the day who wake and take action, they are the dangerous people."

The great mark of the baptism of the Holy Spirit is that we learn to see things that are not. Perceive the impossible, and learn to think out of the box, step out of normality and start seeing life the way God does.

Probably the greatest thing I could say to you is: don't allow your focus to be taken off Him for anything else in the world! Never, never loose sight of the goal and victory. He has done so much for you and me and the best part of this is that it isn't about us, about what we can do or who we are. It's all about Him—what He did, what He has called us to do, and His life-encompassing love!

Perhaps it will take Judgment Day when we see the Master shinning in strength and power, seated on His throne. Before Him from every nation, tribe and tongue, the billions of people whose names were written in the lambs book of life. Perhaps only then will it really sink into us what God's purpose for saving us and putting us on this earth was for, and that living a life wholly committed to Him was worth it all. Perhaps only then will we truly understand the words to one of my favorite hymns, "It will be worth it all when we see Jesus. Life's trials will seem so small when we see Christ. One glimpse of His dear face, all sorrow will erase, so bravely run the race 'till we see Christ."

I have had many failures. I have begun writing books that never made it to the press. I have floundered while witnessing. I have preached dry sermons, prayed pathetic prayers, and made just about every blunder anyone can make. But through it I have learned that the Christian life is a journey of learning, growing, maturing, and pressing forward without ever turning back. And the best part of it is that were running this race *together*, and if we keep our eyes on the goal, and persevere, then we're going to reach the finish line and win the prize together! You are God's instrument to this lost and dying generation, go forth in power and anointing!

My prayer for you is what it says in Philippians 2:15-16 "That you may become blameless and pure, children of God, without rebuke in the midst of a crooked and perverse generation, where you shine like stars in the world holding out the word of life..."

The End

A Big Thank You

To my small, old, Pentium, almost nameless computer, which was a wonderful gift to our family from David and Rachel Murphy.

Thanks to Bill Gates for inventing Microsoft Word (a much easier process for writing a book than a typewriter!)

To Pam Bramlet: Thank you so much for all your help by investing time and effort in this project and for being with me through it every step of the way.

To Darren Crasto: Thank you so much for all your helpful advice in writing.

To Bob and Rose Weiner: This is part of the fruit from the investment you both made in my mom as a teen.

To my dear grandparents, Freeman and Mildred Barnett and Juan y Cecilia Rodriguez: Thank you for all your prayers and for passing down such a Godly heritage to our family.

To Bill Gothard: This book is a product of "Knoxville 2000" when you spoke to the apprenticeship students, telling us to write down all our thoughts and ideas that could give practical help or inspiration to other people. I came home and said, "Mom, I'm going to write a book!"

To Roger and Debbie Audorff and all the YWAM Monterrey "gang": Thank you for always challenging me to be radical for Christ, to hit the mark, and to "Know God and make Him known". You guys are awesome!

To all my friends who were my "guinea pigs." (I tested out everything in the book on them!)

And saving the best for last, to the lover of my soul, Jesus Christ: You are everything to me. You make this life worth living. Give me the power to walk my talk, and the strength to live my whole life in a way that will make it count for You. That I may provoke a smile on Your face and that You may be pleased with me all the days of my life. I want my life to mark a difference in this world that would count for Eternity.

And last but not least, to all those great, godly men and women who have been my role models in life and invested their time and lives into mine, to help me grow spiritually and be more like Jesus.

"The Lord gave the word: and great was the company of those who published it." -Psalm 68:11

About the Author

Born August 23rd 1984, at 4:30 pm, Cristina was 15 years old when she first started writing this book. She is a missionary's daughter who has lived most of her life in Latin America. Being home-schooled has been a great blessing for Cristina since she has had more time to develop other favorite things such as writing, reading, giving flute and English lessons, studying German, playing guitar, and traveling.

Printed in the United States
200132BV00002B/532-546/A